'Much as I didn't expect this, I er⟨...⟩ was refreshing to see some legali⟨...⟩ the most misused and overused te⟨...⟩

Rory Sutherland
Vice-chairman, Ogilvy UK
www.ogilvy.com/uk/

'This book belongs on your shelf. It explains how to develop and protect IP, a brand name, and brand symbols all crucial to long term success and all underappreciated and understudied.'

David Aaker
Vice-chairman, Prophet; brand strategist; author
davidaaker.com

'As marketers we need to hone our skills and keep learning to expand our knowledge. I recommend this book for marketers who want to improve their knowledge and understanding of the application of IP to their work.'

Sophie Devonshire
CEO, The Marketing Society
marketingsociety.com

'Brands are the lifeblood of a business. If you own, or are custodian of, one then you must, must, must protect and nurture its precious equity. This book will give you a head start.'

Phil Barden
Managing Director, DECODE Marketing Ltd;
author of Decoded: The Science Behind Why We Buy

'Your brand is a cornerstone asset and it's worth getting right. This book will make sure you are creating a brand in line with the latest evidence-based thinking on how brands grow and how to develop distinctive brand assets. This book should be a companion for any entrepreneur with ambition to create real value.'

Daniel Priestley
CEO, Dent Global
www.dent.global

'A welcome salve for many a curious soul and a thoroughly enjoyable easy read on two critical subjects for the Digital Age. Hopefully this invigorating book will help change the way marketers, designers, and MBA students are trained in IP, and IP lawyers are trained in branding. Not before time!'

Chrissie Lightfoot
CEO, EntrepreneurLawyer Ltd
entrepreneurlawyer.co.uk

'*Brand Tuned* is essential reading for all entrepreneurs who want to build and protect brands for long term profit and market share. You should read this before you even think about naming a product or designing a logo.'

Joe Gregory
Founder, Rethink Press; author of *Make Your Book Pay*
rethinkpress.com

'Brands are important assets. They take time to build. This book summarizes how we can most effectively build and protect them so we don't waste valuable time and resources. A useful guide, not just for those working in a legal profession.'

Wiemer Snijders
Partner, The Commercial Works; curator of *Eat Your Greens*
www.commercialworks.eu

'Anyone involved with setting up or growing a business will benefit enormously from the insight provided by this book into the world of branding. All aspects are thoroughly covered in a way which is both enjoyably readable and positively instructive.'

Michael Harrison
Chartered patent and trade mark attorney
Past President, Chartered Institute of Patent Attorneys

'In *Brand Tuned*, Shireen Smith brings clarity and focus to the critical concepts of building and protecting brand value.'

Derrick Daye
Branding Strategy Insider

'Shireen Smith has done the branding community and all businesspeople a great service by highlighting the importance of IP law in branding. Who better than a lawyer with branding experience to explain where the two disciplines overlap and dispel some common misconceptions about both.'

Rob Meyerson
Podcast Host, How Brands Are Built
www.howbrandsarebuilt.com

'Well organized and perfectly written, *Brand Tuned* is a bedside book for any entrepreneur who takes their business' journey seriously. It approaches branding not only as naming a company but also as a strategy to help you start your business journey one step ahead. From its cleverly structured methodology to well-presented research, *Brand Tuned* will surely become a guide for small and big scale businesses alike and help light the way for start-ups as well as experienced industry leaders. Knowing her readers' needs thoroughly, Shireen Smith continues to share her valuable experience in the most innovative way possible.'

Levent Yildizgoren
Managing Director, TTC wetranslate Ltd

'Shireen Smith provides an elegant discussion on brands, whose modest length belies the scope of its wisdom and practical advice. Nearly every page offers an insight worth remembering, and she combines her intelligent observations with abundant germane examples. If you are a trademark professional, read this book. If you are a branding or marketing professional, read this book.'

Neil Wilkof
Counsel, Dr. Eyal Bressler
Author of *Trade Mark Licensing*

brand
tuned

The new rules of
branding, strategy and
intellectual property

SHIREEN SMITH

First published in Great Britain by Practical Inspiration Publishing, 2021

© Shireen Smith, 2021

The moral rights of the author have been asserted

ISBN   978-1-78860-269-3   (print)
          978-1-78860-268-6   (epub)
          978-1-78860-267-9   (mobi)

Every effort has been made to trace copyright holders and to obtain their permission for the use of copyright material. The publisher apologizes for any errors or omissions and would be grateful if notified of any corrections that should be incorporated in future reprints or editions of this book.

Contents

Foreword

As I began to prepare for the launch of my new platform, FemPeak, I knew it was imperative to sort out any IP issues as soon as possible. I was already connected to Shireen and was aware that she was a respected intellectual property lawyer specializing in trademarks and brands. So, she seemed the right ally for my new venture, and I began working with her.

I soon discovered that the name I was intending to use was unsuitable. There was a risk that a trademark owner might sue me for using a similar name. Although this was disappointing news, I'm so pleased I discovered the problem early on when I was just getting started. It would have caused untold inconvenience and stress if I had used the name without considering the IP side.

I soon found a different name, FemPeak, and protected it so I can have complete peace of mind that nobody else can lay claim to the name. Another key way my early attention to IP helped is in giving me a process to follow and documents to use whenever I engage help, such as web developers. Like that I know the IP belongs to my company.

As a tech philosopher, film maker, and founder of a digital marketing firm for thought-leaders (Smart Cookie Media), I cannot emphasize enough how important it is to prioritize IP in this digital age. Getting help with IP early on, as I did with FemPeak, sets you up to build your brand on strong foundations.

I'm still in the early phases of my journey with FemPeak, getting the business model right, understanding what people want and need that FemPeak can uniquely offer, getting clearer about my vision, and thinking through my values. Shireen's insight that the founder's philosophy and worldview is the basis of the brand makes complete sense to me, because I too emphasize the fundamental importance of knowing yourself in my book *Career Fear (And How to Beat It)*. If we don't first understand ourselves, how can we articulate what our brand stands for and believes in? How can we know what change we are trying to make in market conditions that our customers will appreciate, if we don't take the time to understand ourselves first? That is the starting point to defining our brand and establishing a winning strategy to grow our business.

Although there are many books on branding, *Brand Tuned* stands out in giving you the whole picture. I like that its ideas build on the latest respected research into how brands grow, and how to develop distinctive brand assets, while also covering intellectual property. Given her extensive experience in the field, Shireen is the right person to write this book, tying in how IP affects branding decisions and its place at the heart and centre of business. She has simplified what is a complex and confused subject.

The book is an eye opener for any business owner or marketer. It's a must read guide on how to create a distinctive brand and build it in a way that is right for you and your business while avoiding potential pitfalls. Knowing what can and cannot be owned, and how to make choices without risk of confusion with other people's brands, is fundamental. I will be guided by the ideas in this book when I decide what digital and other assets to create and how to protect them.

If you're looking to understand what branding involves, and what actions to take to create a strong brand using intellectual property, this book will be your essential resource. Follow the process and clear pathway it outlines in order to take the essential actions to create your brand. It's all in there: how to think through your business and brand to choosing a name, symbol, music, and other brand elements.

Somi Arian

Acknowledgements

I would like to thank the following for discussing branding with me on the podcast and otherwise; their insights shaped my thoughts and ideas in writing this book: Mark Ritson, Adam Morgan, Phil Barden, Rand Fishkin, Chris Radford, Will Critchlow, Anne Chasser, Daniel Greenberg, Giles Edwards, JP Castlin, Stephen Willard, Brad VanAuken, Derrick Daye, John Williams, Chandresh Pala, Bryony Thomas, Susan Payton, David B Horne, Ronnie Fox, Chrissie Lightfoot, Stephen Robertson, Jeremy Miller, Levent Yildizgoren, Alex Hamilton, Simon Banks, and Darlene Hart. I was much inspired by the work of a prominent woman in the branding and marketing space, Sophie Devonshire. Also, thanks to Lucy McCarraher, Joe Gregory, Lucy Werner, and Daniel Priestley, who gave invaluable guidance at various stages of the book. Thank you too to Michael Harrison, Simon Sellars, and Nick Thomas for providing excellent legal support on client work. Without them I would not have found time to write this book. And a special thanks to Camisha Early for her superb support with design and research and to Denise Brady and Edin Mucic, too. This book could not have been written without the guidance of Alison Jones and Becki Bush. Thanks to them and the whole team at Practical Inspiration. And last but not least a special thanks to my husband Paul, and daughters Chloe and Lilia, for being there, supporting me, and even giving feedback on sections of the book.

Introduction

Why should you consider 'brand' as a fundamental cornerstone for your business? Why create one? What is involved in building and developing a strong brand? How do you make your brand stand out? Is it about getting a snazzy logo and beautiful designs? And how does your brand support you to achieve long-term success?

I wanted to write a book to answer these questions and more because, despite having been a business owner since 2005 and a trademark lawyer supporting companies with brand protection, I did not have the answers.

I wanted to find out what was involved in branding a business so I could explain why it is essential to take account of intellectual property (IP) during the process. Having learned about marketing and branding to navigate my own business and having been involved in brand protection work as an IP lawyer for more than 20 years, I had come across companies whose early decisions made their business journey unnecessarily difficult, and even pushed some of them into insolvency. So, I wanted to highlight how to increase the effectiveness of a business by creating its brand with IP as an uppermost consideration.

As I embarked on writing this book, I soon discovered that the branding industry is a minefield with conflicting advice and multiple disciplines, where the role of IP is largely marginalized or misunderstood. Much of the advice about branding is conflicting and impenetrable due to the preponderance of jargon, folklore, hype, and pop psychology. It is widely believed that IP law is about protecting what you have already created, and that protection is a separate exercise to address later if a business succeeds.

When you turn your knowledge and skills into a business and brand, you create IP – so it makes sense to use IP law to guide your decisions. However, as mentioned, the perspective of IP is often missing in branding, even though a brand is often the most important intellectual property a successful business creates since 'brand' affects your revenues and the value of your business.

This led to my decision to create a framework (TUNED) – as an approach for companies to use when building a business and brand, which I will go into in more detail later.

My journey in the world of branding and IP

I have seen the problems that can arise when brands are created without regard to IP, having known many clients, prospective clients, and others in my periphery and network who have been guided wrongly by misinformation around the concepts of brand and IP.

I set up a podcast and interviewed designers, marketers, and entrepreneurs to find out what branding involved for them. What role did the brand play in people's business success? I looked further afield. The theory in academic books on brand management was difficult to apply, I assume because such books are largely written for other academics. Across all the books I considered, there was no clear universal terminology or consensus as to what the essential ingredients are to create an effective brand.

My search for more rigorous, scientific information about brands led to a body of research from the Ehrenberg-Bass

Institute for Marketing Science based at the University of South Australia. Books written by professors from the Institute – namely Byron Sharp's *How Brands Grow* (2010) and Jenni Romaniuk's *Building Distinctive Brand Assets* (2018) – bust many pseudo-science and marketing myths. However, some of their ideas presented further hurdles.

I wanted to highlight the gulf between the worlds of brand protection and brand creation in this book because the misinformation around the concept of brand and intellectual property, and the split between the two worlds, exacerbates the situation: if you do not take proper account of IP laws when creating a brand, it can present a significant problem to achieving affordable and effective branding. To bring the two worlds together involves the need for improved training. It calls for new ground rules on how to create a brand.

To propose some of these new rules, I had to first make sense of several controversies spawned by Byron Sharp's ideas. So, I sought out individuals to talk to who had developed their thinking around these ideas and made sense of concepts that lie at the heart of branding. In this way I developed my own ideas on key areas of controversy. These are outlined in this book.

Why me?

So, who am I to teach you about branding? Well, as an IP lawyer much of my work involves business and brand issues. I am also drawn to creativity. I could just as easily have ended up here via fashion design or architecture, both career options I considered before law.

There is a stereotypical view of lawyers that assumes they are not creative. Lawyers are typically seen as left-brainers

– strong analytical thinkers focused on logic. But the truth is, there is so much need for creative thinking in the practice of law that is frequently overlooked. What's more, neuroscientists have tested the premise that the human brain favours one side over the other[1] using magnetic resonance imaging of 1,000 people. They found that the networks in one side of our brains are not generally stronger than the networks on the other side.

The misconception that you need a creative to support your branding project leads people to turn to designers far too soon. Creating a brand without the right IP and business approach can result in an ineffective, worthless brand. You could quite simply waste your money. The TUNED framework in this book helps you to build the brand of your business the right way.

We all have something driving us, something that attracts us to solve certain problems, to want to improve something in the world, to make a change in particular areas. Branding is the subject I want to contribute to above all others. I am drawn to it because it is both intensely personal and business focused. Decisions about how to design a business and create its brand go to the very heart of who you are as founder. These decisions create the foundations of success.

Equipping you to succeed

While there is no formula for success in business, it is nevertheless the case that certain foundational decisions set you up better than others to succeed. How you design your business

---

[1] 'An evaluation of the left-brain vs. right-brain hypothesis with resting state functional connectivity magnetic resonance imaging', https://journals.plos.org/plosone/article?id=10.1371/journal.pone.0071275

has long-term implications, so think through your ideas correctly so you develop a distinctive brand that stands out in the market.

IP is intrinsic to business. It is not something to identify and protect after you have a thriving business. By then it may be too late. My ambition for this book is to equip anyone interested in developing their brand to approach branding correctly, to learn how to make correct IP decisions along the way.

This book is relevant to leaders who want to understand how to brand their business and take account of IP. Brand matters for every business of any size. Making good decisions entails having good information, which makes reading good books not just a pleasure but a business obligation. Think of this book as an investment for your brand.

To write a book that would be relevant internationally, I only discuss IP at a high level of generality, and spell 'trademark' in the way it is spelled in the USA and online, rather than as two words, which is how it is spelled in UK legal contexts.

Founders with the ambition to build a substantial business and brand can access more guidance than is provided in this book to develop their brand by assessing whether they have what it takes to stand out as the first choice, or 'go to' brand, in their sector. To do this, complete the Brand Tuned scorecard (www.brandtuned.com/scorecard).

How to use this book

If I had so much difficulty wading through the books to understand what branding involves, I doubt founders and businesses would find it easy to work out how to deal with their branding, and who to learn from. This is where the TUNED framework comes in. Built on all my interviews, research, and experience, the framework signposts the order in which to consider issues when structuring and designing your business and brand. It involves thinking about your brand deeply *before* getting its visual identity designed and building the brand. Visual designs come at the end of the process, while deciding your business strategy comes before the brand strategy. I have witnessed business owners who move straight from idea to visual design branding. In the process they fail to think through their business idea deeply enough. The accent must first be on developing a successful business model and formulating a clear brand strategy.

How you read the book is up to you, but I would suggest that the most helpful approach would be to read the book through once quite quickly, and then go back to elements of the TUNED framework that particularly interest you. Depending on the stage you have reached in your business, you might focus on naming your business by going back to part 3. Once you have worked through the book and are ready to commission the visual identity, be sure to read through chapter 4 again. And if you just want to understand the IP dimension of branding, read chapters 2, 3, 4, 8, 9, and 11.

Here is a quick overview of what the book covers:

Chapter 1 explains what brand, branding, and other common terms mean and why 'brand' matters. It sets the scene for how to approach the branding of your business.

Chapter 2 outlines three fundamental problems in branding, specifically what can happen when IP is ignored, untrained service providers offering branding services, and the lack of support for small businesses to manage their brand.

Part 1: 'T' – Think IP first!

Chapter 3 properly introduces the first element of the TUNED framework, namely what IP means, why it matters, and what the 'property' element of the word signifies in practice.

Chapter 4 looks at how buyers notice brands, what to consider when deciding which brand assets to create for your brand, and the role of protection in maintaining your distinctiveness.

Part 2: 'U' – Understand the market

Chapter 5 is all about the importance of thinking about the business concept and developing your strategy for bringing your idea to market. It highlights the importance of considering your vision, mission, values, and purpose and of formulating your business strategy.

Chapter 6 is about thinking through what business you are really in and how to go about doing research to understand customers' wants and needs. Understanding yourself is a key aspect of understanding the market.

Chapter 7 discusses what positioning and differentiation mean, and how the category in which you position your product and service impacts your success. How should you address differentiation in light of Byron Sharp's ideas about distinctiveness and differentiation?

Part 3: 'N' – Name it right

Chapter 8 considers the third component of the TUNED framework, naming. It focuses on naming hierarchies so you can approach naming strategically.

Chapter 9 addresses the importance of brand names and clears up some of the misconceptions that exist. It includes types of names, and an explanation of how trademarks impact your choice of name.

Chapter 10 explains the considerations involved in thinking about your personal, business, and product brands, and some of the criteria you might want to consider when deciding what name to use for your business.

Part 4: 'E' – Establish the brand strategy

Chapter 11 focuses on the fourth component of the TUNED framework, namely establishing your brand strategy. The focus is on how to decide your brand strategy and clarify your brand identity. These are pre-requisites to developing your visual identity.

Part 5: 'D' – Drive the brand strategy

Chapter 12, the final element of the TUNED framework, focuses on how to build the brand once you have created it, what to focus on, and how to allocate your budget between driving sales and building the brand.

Epilogue is a short wrapping-up section.

CHAPTER 1

What is a brand?
Why does it matter?

Like ships passing in the night, it is all too common to have a conversation with someone about brands and branding and make little connection. The terminology is too unclear. Even those who undergo a formal branding process, as I did when I first set up in business on my own, can emerge from the experience no clearer on what 'brand' and 'branding' really mean.

Surprisingly, there is no single accepted definition among experts, so let us start with the origins of branding.

Origins of branding

The word 'brand' has its roots in the identifying mark that was burned on livestock with a branding iron. The original purpose for doing this was so farmers could tell their livestock apart from others. As well as the visual and identification purpose a brand also made a ranch's cattle unique. Sometimes the brand mark told you the name or the symbol of the ranch, or owner of the cattle. If any rustlers stole the cattle, the evidence was right there that they were stolen. In this way, branding served multiple purposes for farmers:

- a legal mark of identification,
- a physical mark of identification,
- a way of linking the cattle to the owner,

- a way to tell cattle apart from those of others, and
- a source of prestige for the ranch.

Just looking at the branded livestock enabled people to distinguish them from other cattle. You were also able to see the connection between them and the farmer or the ranch. People knew who the very strong, numerous, and healthy cattle belonged to. 'Those are Mr Miller's cattle. He owns five thousand cattle and one of the biggest ranches around. See how healthy his cattle are? That must be a big ranch to own all that livestock.'

A brand mark discouraged cattle thieves. It would be like stealing a company car with the logo and the owner's name on it.

Brands or trademarks also identified the source of the olive oil or wine contained in ancient Greek amphoras and created value in the eyes of the buyers by building a reputation for the producer or distributor of the oil or wine.

Defining 'brand' in business today

So, the origins of branding are all about identification, ownership, and worth. Does that hold true today?

Nowadays, when asked to define a brand, people might quote Jeff Bezos saying that 'your brand is what people say when you're not in the room' or they will say 'everything you do is your brand'. Such statements, in my experience, do more to confuse and obfuscate than to clarify what a brand is.

When I was writing my first book, *Legally Branded,* in 2011, I asked around to see what this word that everyone bandied around so much actually meant to people. The best replies I received at the time were:

- A brand is the face and soul of an organization.
- A brand is more than personality, more than reputation, more than a promise, it is the distinctive DNA of a business.

Wally Olins, a thought leader in brands and branding, defines 'brand' in his *Brand Handbook* (2008):

A brand is simply an organisation, or a product, or a service with a personality… Branding can encapsulate both big and important and apparently superficial and trivial issues simultaneously… Branding is not only a design and marketing tool, but it should also influence everybody in your company; it's a coordinating resource because it makes the corporation's activities coherent and above all, it makes the strategy of the organisation visible and palpable for all audiences to see.

I also consulted authoritative texts, such as *The New Strategic Brand Management: Advanced Insights and Strategic Thinking* (2012) by JN Kapferer, which set out the internationally agreed legal definition of a brand: 'a sign or set of signs certifying the origin of a product or service and differentiating it from the competition'.

The brand name is often the primary way in which consumers identify products and services and is the 'sign' that you would expect customers to use to distinguish your goods and services from those of competitors. Other signs that identify a business include the logo, icon, and tagline – but which of these make up a brand? Can you have a brand without any of them?

Brand vs. product or service or business

In this book, we use the words brand, business, product, or service interchangeably sometimes. It is worth bearing in mind, though, that they do mean different things: your business is your company – the organization that produces your products and services and that makes offers. The business will offer products and services that may or may not be known by separate names. Your brand is the identity and reputation that your business projects – the way consumers perceive your business. In this book, the context often makes it clear whether the distinction is important.

Academic brand experts quibble over the 'right' definition of a brand.

There are two broad camps. One places a stronger emphasis on the relationship that customers have with the brand, as the dominant element of the definition, while the other emphasizes the monetary value created by the brand. However, both camps agree that these two elements are significant. Essentially, the brand is how you create attachment, loyalty, and willingness to buy your products and services.

Whatever the 'correct' theoretical definition of 'brand', I find it easier and more helpful to explain what 'brand' means in a more relatable and practical way. Let us take it out of the abstract and consider an analogy to people's personality and reputation. A brand, whatever else it may be, is an identity – so it is helpful to think about how we form an impression about individuals, how we conjure them up in our minds when talking about them, and then apply those same principles to business branding.

When we encounter an individual, the overall impression we form about them is made up of a combination of characteristics or qualities. Feeding into this combination are that individual's distinctive identity, their character and personality. As people, we all have a name, a way of dressing, talking, and behaving. We are known for topics we tend to talk about. We have our own distinct physical appearance, beliefs and opinions, and style. Some of us are high energy, others laugh a lot or might be rather serious, some are outgoing, while others are introverted. Gradually, as we get to know someone, we see different sides to them, and form a sense of who they are. We might even be able to predict how they will respond in certain situations, whether they can be trusted to see something through, or are likely to give up half-way, and so on.

We have a mental picture and associations when a person's name is mentioned. What we think about them derives from a mixture of our impressions of them: it might include their name, physical appearance, our sense of who they are, what makes them tick, how they make us feel. That is their reputation – or, for our purposes, their brand – although in everyday life we do not tend to say we like someone's brand! Instead, we might say we like their personality. This is shorthand for everything we know and feel about an individual – and when you consider the same thing about a business instead of a person, we call it their brand.

A brand, then, is a perception. It is a territory in the mind of your customers. You can try to influence and define it in positive ways. It is the impression we form of a business through our experiences of it. When we hear a company's name that we have previously come across, certain associations might come to mind. The name triggers our memories. The memories might encompass their products or services, interactions we had with the company's representatives, the customer service we received, and so on. What the business says on its website and in content on its blog, videos, and social media posts, and how the business is run in terms of the quality of its products and services and customer service: the totality of experiences of the business go to create the overall impression the world forms about the business. That is what people mean when they say everything you do is your brand, or that every business has a brand whether they know it or not.

As you become more known as a business, you will evoke a certain response in others. Just as with an individual, there will not be a universal feeling or impression about their brand, but there will be some commonalities; some things about them that most people would agree on. In the same way, your business will be noticed by customers and others in a particular way. Although you might try to influence the perception people have of your brand, ultimately your brand is what customers perceive it to be.

Too small to have a brand?

Some business owners believe that the concept of brand does not apply to them, because their business is small. They believe that only well-known household-name businesses have brands, that different rules apply to small businesses than to household-name brands, and that case studies about well-known brands are not relevant to them.

Yet all the big businesses we know today started out as small ones. The businesses that are now household names started out as a product or service that met a market need. With the passage of time those businesses have acquired widespread market recognition for the products and services they provide. They have managed their brands well and built them, so they are now well known. Good brands do not emerge by pure chance. It takes active management of a brand, as the business gets off the ground, to build the brand.

Some brands are just less well known than others. Some may be well known to a micro community and others may not be known yet because they are just getting started. If you are thinking big in the business, then it is never too soon to start considering the brand you want to create.

Designing a business brand identity

One key difference between a personal brand and a business brand, of course, is that people have an existing personality. Their background, values, and beliefs impact their personal brand. While it is possible to manage your personal brand – that is, to control the face you present to the world – by choosing how much to reveal about yourself, and what topics you publicly talk about, it is generally not possible to package an individual up to appear in a completely new light. In other words, people are not blank slates in the way a business can be when it is first started.

A newly created business has no background or history. It will develop a brand that you influence.

What the brand stands for, what it is to be known for, and what brand promise it will make are essential issues to think through, as discussed in this book.

And here is the important thing: rather than letting your brand evolve haphazardly, and get a reputation randomly over time, you should impact the direction of the brand by designing the business intentionally. You can influence the perceptions about your business by thinking deeply about your aims for creating the business. The brand will be impacted by your values and purpose, what you stand for and believe. Your hope is that the brand develops over time and acquires the reputation you would want it to have.

Managing your brand carefully should be an active part of your business journey because branding is not a one-off event you do and forget. It runs through everything you do as you build your business. Not every business will achieve brand status in the sense of becoming a known provider for a group of consumers. While every business may be described as a brand, using the word in its loosest sense, to truly be an effective brand means your name alone acquires pulling power – even if that might be just within a small community initially.

Design is not just how a brand looks

Design is about how the business works, not just how it looks. As Steve Jobs put it: 'Some people think design means how it looks. But if you dig deeper it's really how it works'.[2]

---

[2] https://www.idrlabs.com/quotes/steve-jobs.php

In this book, when we talk about business or brand design, this is what it means. We are talking design in its widest sense, to denote *how something works*. Where we do need to talk about how something looks, we will use the phrase 'visual design' instead – hopefully, this will make the distinction quite clear.

Even though people readily agree that a brand is more than a logo, their actions are often not aligned with their words. I see it happening again and again. One of the first steps people take when they have a new idea is to ask for recommendations for designers and creative agencies. It seems to be ingrained in our society to associate branding with visual design. I suggest people consciously restrain themselves from turning to visual designs when they are ready to create a brand. Certainly, I had to stop myself going straight to a designer when I began making some changes in my business in 2019/2020. Instead, I realized that I needed to first design the business and brand, and do some thinking without focusing on the visual dimension. It would have actually distracted my thinking to consider the visual design immediately.

While visual design matters in supporting the overall impression and feelings a brand evokes and conveys, if you do not first focus on what the brand stands for, its point of view and brand promise, and how you will meet a market need and create a successful business, then no amount of visual identity design will turn your business into a brand. Branding is about substance, it is not just about surface imagery, important though that imagery might be. Remember the analogy I drew earlier between a person and a business' brand? What someone looks like is part of the overall impression we form about them, but there are a host of other factors that create a person's identity. The same goes for a business' brand.

Design is not just about reputation and image

While companies are very sensitive about their reputation and image, the brand is not synonymous with reputation and image in the same way that it is not synonymous with a logo. Reputation management as a concept is an overly defensive concept, resulting in an over-prudent approach to decision-making. It focuses on not making waves for fear of damaging the company's reputation. This is not in keeping with the concept of brand as a champion of the values the business stands for. Designing a brand is not a protective, passive activity – you do not design a thing to stay the same – it is an active, positive living thing. Designing a brand goes beyond being well regarded by everybody; it is about having a *point of view*.

Although we may say we are launching a brand, in fact we launch a product or service in the hope that an effective brand will develop. Eventually, that product or service may evoke the brand associations we aim for. With the passage of time, the brand becomes like an unwritten contract between the business and the customer: this is what is meant by the phrase 'brand promise'. The brand must keep its identity, and permanently increase its relevance. It must be loyal to itself, to its mission, and to its clients. Each brand is free to choose its values, purpose, and positioning, but once these have been chosen and advertised, they become the benchmark for customer satisfaction. The prime determinant of customer satisfaction is the gap between customers' experiences and their expectations. The brand's positioning sets up these expectations. If the brand meets their expectations, the name commands trust, respect, and even engagement.

Defining 'branding'

So, if a *brand* is a name that influences buyers, *branding* is the activity of defining and developing that brand. It is the activity of determining the brand's identity, what it stands for and believes. It is about how to transform the product category with the product and acquire recognition in the market. It is working out what the brand stands for and mobilizing all a company's internal resources to set itself apart from its competitors. All the elements mentioned above and more – such as the customer journey and how you answer the phone, every detail, including creating the visual identity for your brand – are what branding encompasses. It is the process by which you put your best strategic thinking into defining and developing your brand. By working out your business philosophy and how you intend the business to function, you gradually work out your brand. Get some coaching support if this would help your thinking.

Once you have clarity about the brand you want to create, and have established your brand strategy, you would turn your thinking into visual designs to give your business a visual identity and brand name that evoke your desired brand. Your visual designs provide your company with a face, and help buyers distinguish your business from others. This supports your marketing and advertising efforts by enabling consumers to recognize you again if they have come across your brand in the past. How to approach the visual identity so your business stands out and is remembered is important to take on board before commissioning a creative agency to support your branding.

People often wrongly assume branding is what the marketing and communications team deal with. They place too much, if not exclusive, attention on designs and marketing activity.

Branding is about so much more than this. It needs to start with you as the founder or leader of your organization. It requires a long-term, strategic approach to transform products and services into a brand.

Branding vs. marketing

People buy branded products or services, but branding is not a substitute for marketing. Both are needed.

Marketing is quite different to branding. It is the activity you engage in to bring a product or service to market; sending out branded messages and communications. So, marketing overlaps with branding – but is distinct.

Marketing aims at forecasting the needs of specific consumer segments and drives the business to tailor products and services to these needs. The right marketing support is essential when you are introducing a new product or service into the market. It helps you to understand the market and avoid wasting time creating a product that may not meet customers' needs. Branding is *everything* you do to bring your brand to life once you have decided what product or service to introduce and have tested the market. It determines what your brand stands for, what your product looks like, and what kind of vibe it gives.

Take home messages

- A brand is the impression we form of a business through our experiences of it.
- Your brand will be impacted by your values and purpose.
- Work out your business philosophy and how you intend the business to function, to gradually work out your brand.
- Branding is the activity of defining and developing a brand; make this an active part of your business journey.
- Create a name and visual designs that evoke your desired brand.

CHAPTER 2

The three fundamental problems in branding

Now that we know what branding means, it is time to look at how branding services can be unpredictable sometimes. Apart from the fact that the terms brand and branding are poorly understood by business owners, there are broadly three issues:

- Ignoring IP from the start
- Untrained service providers
- A lack of support for small business

Ignoring IP from the start

The internet has made it very easy to start a business; you can form a company, register your domain, buy templates for your business, hire freelancers or agencies to support your branding and marketing – and away you go with your business idea. There has been a vast increase in the number of businesses as a result. One aspect of this is that legal advice is often missed. People assume they just need lawyers to draft agreements or to register rights like trademarks for them. For many SMEs (small and medium-sized enterprises), qualified legal advice seems to be replaced with Google searches. While this is great for accessibility, it has its downsides. The big problem with relying on Google search results for advice is that you do not know what you don't know – and if you don't know what knowledge you are missing, then how can you search for it? And how do you know if the search results you find are appropriate to your circumstances?

I suspect if a study were undertaken of the many businesses that fail every year, we would find a large number were due to not taking on board an important IP issue. There is a widespread lack of clarity about the limits of copyright and IP laws, which leads to problems for businesses that do not understand what names they may adopt or what materials they may or may not freely use. We will look at IP more closely in the next chapter. A common mistake concerns the choice of name. We will look at naming in much more depth in part 3.

Here is an example. In one case I came across, an entrepreneur had spent £100,000 of his own money creating a new online business. He had a fantastic visual identity and website created for his new business by an agency. He was spending thousands of pounds monthly on social media marketing and advertising to get traction for his new venture. Then he hit a problem: the market leader in his industry initiated a domain dispute on the grounds that the domain name he was using was similar to their own brand name. The upshot was that his domains were permanently confiscated, and he had to start over with a new name. All the money he had spent getting search engine recognition for this domain was lost. Unsurprisingly, his business never recovered from this setback and folded shortly afterwards.

It is important to take IP into account when creating a business or brand, and if you are investing serious money in a project, it is *essential* to do so, to avoid pitfalls like this. Turning ideas, knowledge, and skills into a business involves many IP decisions, so it makes sense to start there before investing in websites, brands, and marketing.

By any other name

The reason the entrepreneur in that example suffered so needlessly is that he did not realize that using a similar name to a competitor is a complete no-no. There is a common misconception that you can simply add a descriptor to a name or change it slightly to co-exist with another brand. It is unclear why this misconception exists, because surely everyone would agree that if another business came along and offered luxury watches and called itself Rolax instead of Rolex, they might be confused – yet for some reason, people assume a different rule applies to them when they are choosing a name!

Untrained service providers

A major flaw in the branding industry today is that it includes such a wide range of companies making service offerings involving branding services. You would think that more choice would be better for clients – but actually, the barriers to entry into this industry are very low. Any new media company offering something customers need, such as websites or social media marketing, could and does decide to support their clients with branding as well – like a bolt-on for their primary product or service.

You can look at this range of companies like a scale. At one end of the scale are completely unqualified service providers whose main service is not branding. They treat it as an add-on service and offer logo and visual design work. This kind of company might include web design companies, marketers, and advertising, social media, or digital marketing agencies, as well as content marketers, graphic designers, product designers, and the like. At the other extreme, there are highly experienced branding professionals who run agencies that specialize in branding, although even these have a mish-mash of styles and approaches.

The plethora of service providers in the market makes it difficult for consumers to know what they are buying when they buy a branding service. There is no outward sign for consumers to be able to tell whether an agency they are intending to use understands branding and IP or not. Most business owners will understandably assume that any creative service provider they use for branding activities knows everything pertinent to the topic, including the law. But it is not part of a designer's or marketer's skillset to know IP law. Indeed, many of them have a poor knowledge of it, and due to the complexity of IP, a little knowledge can be a dangerous thing.

Here is an example. Recently, I came across a designer giving very clear, very emphatic… and unfortunately very wrong advice to her client in an online forum we all had access to. The client had asked a general question about trademarking brand names, and in response, the designer insisted that you cannot trademark a word in general use unless you make it up; she elaborated that trademarking a word like 'Evo-Stick' or 'Twix', that's ok – but that you can't trademark an ordinary word, otherwise no one else would be able to use it in everyday language without being sued. She went on to state, very confidently, that you can trademark an image but that it has to be '20% different from anything else that exists'. She was quite unaware of the misinformation she was conveying about what can and cannot constitute a brand name. In fact, you can trademark an ordinary word, and there is no rule that says you can only trademark an image if it is 20% different from anything else that exists.

On another occasion I observed a designer remarking that she had named more than 50 businesses. She then mentioned that thousands of UK companies use the word Apple, that they just add something to it to make it 'theirs'... so Apple Accounting etc. The implication was that this was an appropriate approach to naming. Whatever the reason for her saying this, it was misleading: famous marks like Apple enjoy broader protection than ordinary marks, in view of its widespread reputation and name recognition. If you pick a famous brand's name such as Apple, that company can stop you from using your name down the line even if you are in a completely different industry. Big companies like Apple are busy enforcing their trademark rights against all manner of problems, including counterfeits. They have bigger issues to address than to tackle every insignificant business that is using their name. However, if such a business ever amounts to anything, and comes to their attention, they are likely to receive an unwelcome reaction, and to be required to rebrand.

Currently, trained marketers and designers receive little to no training in IP. This is a serious problem; the presence of a trained brand manager or marketer heading up an agency does not signify that the service provider has the knowledge it needs to offer certain types of branding service, such as naming. In my ideal world, providers offering a branding service, especially if they also name businesses, should have training in IP or should involve trademark lawyers in the brand creation process. Studies[3] indicate that 96% of all businesses are micro businesses, that is, businesses employing fewer than 10 people, while approximately 4% employ between 10 and 250 employees. This means that 99.9% of businesses, that is some six million businesses, are SMEs. Few of these are likely to have in-house capability to understand IP. Yet the training of marketing and design professionals assumes they will be working with the tiny minority of businesses that have lawyers to advise them on IP. So, seasoned professionals are left to pick up the IP skills they need through experience, and there is no outward sign by which consumers can tell one professional apart from another. Nor can the professional know whether there are any serious gaps in their knowledge.

---

[3] According to official UK government statistics (House of Commons Library, 'Business statistics', Briefing Paper No. 06152, https://researchbriefings.files.parliament.uk/documents/SN06152/SN06152.pdf and Department for Business, Energy & Industrial Strategy (BEIS), 'Business population estimates for the UK and regions 2020: statistical release', www.gov.uk/government/statistics/business-population-estimates-2020/business-population-estimates-for-the-uk-and-regions-2020-statistical-release-html), 96% of all businesses are micro businesses, i.e. small businesses employing fewer than 10 people. Those employing 10 to 250 employees take that number to 99.9%. This demographic, collectively referred to as small and medium-sized enterprises, amounts to some six million businesses in the UK. The remaining 0.1% of businesses are large businesses, employing more than 250 people each. They amount to just 8,000 in total, and yet account for 40% of employment and 48% of turnover. Other reports I have seen indicate that the figures in the USA and Europe are comparable to those in the UK.

A lack of specific support for small businesses

In large businesses there is usually a brand management function so that a brand manager helps choose external suppliers
and co-ordinates with various teams across the organization to
implement the organization's brand strategy and promote sales.
They will need a good level of knowledge of what branding
entails, in order to recognize when to involve various depart-
ments and disciplines. For example, if the company decides to
alter aspects of the brand, such as its name or visual identity,
a good brand manager will know enough about trademarks to
involve the legal department early on. Whether the company
needs packaging changes, product designs, creative advertising, marketing campaigns, IT to enhance the website, or legal,
regulatory, or IP advice, such as to clear a proposed symbol: it
is the job of the brand manager to know which skills are needed
to achieve the company's objectives.

SMEs lack this essential function. Founders and the organization's leaders need to fulfil the role themselves by default. The
problem with this is that they often do not themselves know
enough about business and law to recognize what they need
to do. They are not well placed to know what really matters to
their bottom line when it comes to establishing their brand and
undergoing a visual branding exercise.

If there were a brand management style advisory service for
business, companies would have a way to get guidance when
creating their brands and selecting professionals to support
them with their visual identity and other brand-building needs.

That is where Brand Tuned comes in. It was created to meet
the need I see for brand management support for companies
that need guidance on branding and IP. It is a bridge between
branding activities and brand protection. Ultimately, I believe that

a new breed of professional is needed for this role: an impartial source of support. They should not stand to benefit in offering services such as trademark registration. Nor should they offer visual design or marketing services themselves. Their role should be purely advisory – one of mentoring, coaching, and education. They might then refer clients to lawyers, designers, advertising agencies, and others for their various needs around brand creation, brand building, and marketing – a sort of consul-tant brand manager if you will. For now, though, I hope that this book will start to fill that gap for you!

Take home messages

- You need to take IP into account when creating your business or brand (especially if you are investing serious money in it).
- It is not part of a designer's or marketer's skillset to know IP law.
- Brand managers in large organizations will know when to involve the legal department.
- The SMEs that make up 99.9% of all UK businesses lack in-house branding and legal specialists.
- Brand Tuned provides brand management support for companies that need guidance on branding and IP.

Part 1

t u n e d

Think IP first

In this part, we will explore what IP is all about, and why it is so crucial to consider it at the very beginning of your branding journey.

CHAPTER 3

IP and branding

In chapter 2, we touched on three pitfalls in branding, which included not taking account of IP early on. In this chapter we consider what IP involves in practice.

IP, as it relates to branding, covers many aspects of a project or campaign. As you turn your knowledge, ideas, and skills (often informally referred to as 'your IP') into tangible form, you consider issues and make choices. These issues and choices might include:

- Who to reveal your ideas to
- What name to use
- Whether your idea is protectable, and if so how
- What slogan or tagline to use
- How to design a product or its packaging to stand out
- What music or distinctive sounds to associate with the brand
- What photographs, illustrations, and imagery to use
- What colours, fonts, or logo to use
- Whether to use a symbol or character icon and if so which
- What copy to use for the website, or in advertising
- What scripts to use for videos
- What look and feel to have for your brand or website
- How to use your skills and knowledge in an innovative way

- How to launch an unusual business model
- How to legally protect your business

All these choices and more are impacted by IP laws – because almost all of them invariably involve the creation of intellectual property.

Copying is so rife in business that, if you have a profitable niche or concept, it would be surprising if competitors did not sooner or later try to capture some of your market share. They will borrow freely from other businesses that they believe have identified lucrative market opportunities. They will often copy elements of your branding. Be aware of this, know the difference between what is acceptable, legitimate competition and what is unlawful and unethical. And protect your most valuable assets against damaging copying if you want to maintain your brand's distinctiveness.

Key IP terms and concepts

IP is an umbrella term. Let us pause here to look at the fundamental parts of it.

A **patent** protects the way an invention works – meaning during the term of the patent (a maximum of 20 years), no one can copy how you made your product so that theirs works the same way.

Design rights cover the visual look of your product. Design rights are available where the visual design has a novel element to it, and could cover a wide range of goods, such as handbags or shapes of packaging, and so on. It is even possible to get a design registration for a logo.

Patents and designs are not of central relevance to every business, because these situations do not arise as a matter of course. You can perfectly happily get along in business without ever inventing a patentable product or designing something visual that needs protecting with design registration. Yet people often assume that IP is all about patents.

On the other hand, the core IP rights of trademarks, copyright, and confidential information are relevant to *every* business.

Confidential information we will come to later in this chapter.

Trademarks are how the law protects many brand elements that identify a business as the source or origin of goods and services. Trademarks are how names and slogans are protected (not copyright law). Trademarks are used to protect unique branding elements such as shapes, colours, musical jingles, or even smells. Trademarks are one of the most important IP rights to understand in relation to brands.

Copyright is of universal applicability so should be understood. In the context of a brand, it is relevant to various creations of the mind such as written materials, music, art, logos, and computer programs, to name a few. Remember, the key thing about copyright is that it protects the *expression* of an idea – not the idea itself.

Websites, apps, and other software consist of a whole host of different elements, each of which is protected by different IP rights – generally copyright. Let us look quickly at just one example: a website is a bundle of software, graphics, audio, data, video, and written content, packaged together under a domain name. Many of these individual elements could potentially be in different ownership, and then separately there is the copyright in the underlying code that allows the site to function.

These three core IP rights are universally applicable – the laws are global, thanks to international treaties like the Berne Convention. This also means that IP terminology is similar the world over (although there are some variations in the termi-nology around patents and designs in the USA and Europe). This means that the IP actions you need to take are similar whichever country you are in. The details of the law will differ, of course, but the overall approach to IP will have a strong simi-larity across jurisdictions. So, no matter where you are located, the information about IP that you will glean from this book will be relevant to you. You can then seek out further information and advice in your own country to ensure you take the right actions for your business.

The intangible nature of IP

'Property' is a term that refers to anything we have 'legal title' over, be it a tangible thing like land, a house, a car, or furni-ture; or an intangible thing such as an invention or a brand or a website. The person who has the legal title to something is the owner with enforceable rights in it by law. That means the law can be used against someone who misuses property, such as copying it without permission.

The owner of property is the one with exclusive rights to exploit the property; that is, to grant permissions to others to use that property. This is all tangible and easy to understand so far.

However, I suspect that one reason people overlook IP is that it is somewhat of an intangible concept. You own a book, but unless you wrote the book you certainly will not own the copyright that exists in that book. You merely have the right to read the book.

To bring it into the business world: your business may have a logo, or a website. Unless you create the logo and website yourself or have a written agreement from the creator saying that you own the copyright in them, you merely have a licence to use them for the purpose of your business. However, you will not own the copyright in them.

When you own the property right in something, it means you are the one who has the right to grant permission to use it. So, it is good practice to make sure you own the IP rights in assets that are created for your business, such as logos, websites, and written content. The benefit of ownership is easy to explain by analogy to owning a tangible thing like a house. The owner of a house can let others use that house and charge them a fee to do so. You can let out the entire house or a room inside the house. Again – all straightforward so far. But the same applies to IP: you can do a similar thing with intangibles by granting a *licence* to others.

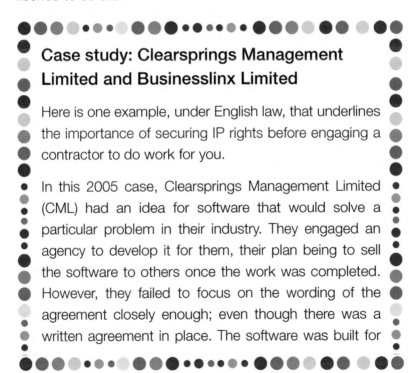

Case study: Clearsprings Management Limited and Businesslinx Limited

Here is one example, under English law, that underlines the importance of securing IP rights before engaging a contractor to do work for you.

In this 2005 case, Clearsprings Management Limited (CML) had an idea for software that would solve a particular problem in their industry. They engaged an agency to develop it for them, their plan being to sell the software to others once the work was completed. However, they failed to focus on the wording of the agreement closely enough; even though there was a written agreement in place. The software was built for them and paid for by them, but ownership of the IP remained with the developers. CML made the classic error of failing to ensure that copyright was assigned to them in the legal agreement with the developer. It discovered, too late, that it had nothing to sell. They merely had a licence to use the software in their own business. As the developers owned the rights in the software, they were free to market and sell it.

The takeaway from this case is that it is crucial to find out how IP ownership passes to you, and how IP impacts your plans *before* you engage anyone to do work on your projects, including on your branding. The example relates to software, but it could apply equally to any other asset. Consult lawyers in your own country to protect yourself just as you would if you were buying land.

The difference between property rights in physical things, like houses, and rights in intangibles, such as a piece of music, content, or software or a name, is that you are constrained by the physical space in your property. You can only let out the property to one person at a time. With an IP asset that you have ownership of, you can potentially license it to many other people in return for royalty payments. You remain the owner and can let an unlimited number of people use it – there are no physical limitations because the property is not a physical thing.

J.K. Rowling of Harry Potter fame is now a successful writer with one of the most valuable brands in the world. In less than 25 years she has become a very rich woman. Her considerable wealth originates from the copyright in her books because their success led to the opportunity to exploit her other IP rights. For example, she granted rights to film producers, merchandising companies, and others. Licensing is the primary source of her wealth rather than book sales. Each time a company produces goods bearing Harry Potter characters on them, J.K. Rowling gets paid.

You would need to grant a licence to a third party if you decided to license or franchise your business. That involves giving permission to them to use your IP assets, such as your name, logo, or know-how. The starting point, therefore, of exploiting your IP assets is to make sure you own the IP in your intangible assets. You are then free to give permissions in many different contexts, such as to license or franchise your business. If you were selling your business, then the buyer would want to find out what you owned, and that would affect the price of your business depending on the assets involved.

How legal rights work as a deterrent

If you have strong enforceable legal rights, competitors (especially those who know what they are doing) will steer clear of deliberately copying your assets. They would not expose themselves to lawsuits and hefty damages claims, knowing they have a poor chance of defending their position. On the other hand, when your legal foundations are weak, competitors know that they can copy and ignore your limited rights because they realize that enforcing your rights will be risky for you. You could lose.

It might be tempting to believe that it is money and resources, not the law, that dictates who wins disputes. While it is true that fighting legal battles can take a lot of time and resource, it is not true that just because a business is bigger it can automatically get its own way. For example, in a recent UK case between Bentley Clothing and Bentley the owners of the famous car brand, Bentley Clothing was able to use the legal process to stop Bentley cars from using the name Bentley on its clothing line. Bentley cars was forced to destroy its entire stock as a result. This is just one example of how owning strong IP rights puts you in a strong position no matter who you are up against. There are countless cases where people with strong IP rights have fought their corner and won.

On the other hand, if a company is bigger and more affluent than you, they know that you will lack the funds to devote a substantial budget to fighting your case and are less likely to do so if your rights are weak. After all, it could be a futile exercise. They take what is yours, and often you will be the one that has to rebrand because it is cheaper than fighting your case.

The moral of the story? Do not let reservations about the affordability of legal disputes to defend your IP rights stop you from protecting those rights in the first place. The fact that you are a small brand with limited resources is added reason why you should focus on choosing assets such as names and signs that are inherently strong from a legal perspective and protecting them. Often, simply owning strong IP assets is enough to avoid disputes arising.

Not securing your IP is more, rather than less, likely to result in litigation for your business. Litigation is extremely expensive, and therefore reducing the risk of it is far more important for small businesses than for the large household-name brands that occupy the news. This means choosing your brand assets well and engaging with IP early.

No amount of protection will help you if the choice is a poor one.

To whom to reveal your ideas: confidentiality and sharing ideas

As we now know, ideas are not protected by copyright – only the expression of an idea is. This means that important intellectual assets that might give a business a competitive advantage, such as its know-how, trade secrets, and ideas, are only protected by IP law while they are kept *confidential*. If confidential information is stolen or leaked, then your remedy is to bring a legal action against whoever misused that information. This can be challenging, though, and, in practice, it is more prudent to manage your confidential information to reduce the risk of it getting into the wrong hands than it is to rely on legal action once your information has lost its confidential status. The damage will have already been done by then.

Think of confidential information as if it were something like the location of buried treasure. That knowledge would clearly be valuable information; you would know not to freely divulge it if you wanted to ensure the treasure remained untouched by others. In the same way, all businesses have know-how and trade secrets that they need to be mindful of before disclosing. If you must disclose the information as part of a course or programme you offer, then there should be confidentiality provisions in the terms under which you give access to it.

Canny competitors stand to benefit from insights they glean from you, if you are not careful. Let us now look at three case studies that demonstrate the importance of confidentiality.

Case study: Coca-Cola

If you have an idea that could be patented, you need to take care not to discuss the idea with anyone, unless they are a professional adviser like your lawyer, or unless you have a confidentiality agreement in place. This is because if you do discuss the idea outside a context of confidentiality, the idea is deemed to be in the public domain, and the law will only grant a patent over ideas and concepts that are not already known.

Coca-Cola could have patented its recipe 100 years or so ago. Instead, it decided not to do so and to keep it a secret. Reportedly, they maintain a strict policy of confidentiality to safeguard their secret recipe. They have even built a story around that decision, so that the secret recipe has become part of their brand story. Apparently, only three people in the organization at any one time ever have access to the formula. The company has put in place an elaborate method to safeguard the recipe.

Before you reveal your ideas and innovation, keep your ideas close to your chest and do not rely too much on NDAs (non-disclosure agreements). Remember: your aim should be to protect the secret information rather than to have someone to sue if your information gets out into the public domain. Knowing what to keep to yourself and what to freely reveal involves understanding the commercial value of ideas, information, and insights, and is a key aspect of IP.

Case study: Apple and Steve Jobs

Steve Jobs paid a lot of attention to secrecy in the organization to ensure products were kept under wraps until launch. He kept a tight grip on confidential information. Internal secrecy within Apple was as stringent and as strictly adhered to as would be the case in military organizations.

Swift punishment of employees and managers followed if Jobs' own version of the military code was not strictly complied with. In the book *Beyond Strategy: The Impact of Next Generation Companies* (2014), Michael Moesgaard Andersen and Flemming Poulfelt describe how the Apple organization worked. Apparently, there were silos within silos, and security badges to ensure that employees were only allowed in certain areas. Only a few Apple employees ever saw the most restrictive area, the industrial design lab where Apple's designers worked. Employees were kept in the dark as much as possible. Steve Jobs was often the only person within the organization who could see the big picture. Others just had access to what they needed to know.

As a result of this internal policy, the iPhone exploded onto the market out of nowhere and took the industry by surprise.

Case study: Guiltless Gourmet and Frito-Lay

In the book *Brand Failures: The Truth About the 100 Biggest Branding Mistakes of All Time* (2005), Matt Haig mentions Guiltless Gourmet, a small business success story in the 1990s. The company made baked, low-fat tortilla chips, which were endorsed as healthy by the US Center for Science in the Public Interest. The company had evolved in the space of five years from being a home-based operation into a US $23 million business with a massive factory.

Frito-Lay, one of the largest US companies producing snack-food, was at one point interested in buying Guiltless Gourmet but, for reasons that are unclear, never went ahead with the purchase. Apparently, as a result of the (ultimately unsuccessful) buy-out talks, Frito-Lay may have gained access to Guiltless Gourmet's information. Not only that, but the founder of Guiltless Gourmet reportedly went and worked with Frito-Lay as a consultant!

Guiltless Gourmet's most important asset was its recipe. A competitor is well placed to quickly understand and take advantage if it gets access to a piece of such information. It is very risky therefore to have buy-out talks with competitors for a business such as Guiltless Gourmet.

Was the founder of Guiltless Gourmet aware that his success would breed competition? That his company's meteoric rise within a niche product category was inevitably going to catch the attention of a larger rival, and that Frito-Lay's well-established distribution network posed a serious risk? This is what I mean when I say that IP involves being aware of the *value of information*. That alone should have been a reason to avoid giving Frito-Lay access to any of its secret recipes.

As it happened, Guiltless Gourmet probably equipped Frito-Lay to produce a new product – low-fat Baked Tostitos – which was soon available in supermarkets across the United States thanks to Frito-Lay's sizeable distribution network. Straightaway, Frito-Lay's offering was eating into Guiltless Gourmet's market share. Within a year, Guiltless Gourmet's revenues reduced to US $9 million, and the company was forced to shut down its factory and start outsourcing. Its workforce slimmed down from 125 to 10 employees.

Frito-Lay is reported as saying that 'Guiltless Gourmet provided us with a great benchmark to get our product better-tasting'.

When you are insufficiently aware of the value of your IP you could let your own brand down. Guiltless Gourmet seems to have given away the secrets of the company to a dangerous competitor because they failed to understand IP.

IP myths and misinformation

Hopefully now you have a better understanding of what IP is, and are ready to start 'thinking IP first' when it comes to creating your brand. Before we do so, though, let us take a look at some of the most common myths that surround branding and IP.

1. Copyright is secured by posting a copy of your work to yourself.

I have often come across advice, even sometimes from business lawyers, which says that all you need to do to establish proof of your ownership of copyright is to put the evidence in an envelope and post it to yourself, making sure there is a clear postmark on the envelope establishing the date of its posting. This is referred to as poor man's copyright. Unfortunately, it is completely wrong advice! The courts certainly would not accept such a document as adequate proof of copyright; for a start, the envelope could have been tampered with after posting. In the UK the best way to establish proof of the date on which a copyright work was created is to use a statutory declaration, which is a form of oath to which you attach copies of your work and swear before a solicitor or commissioner for oaths. In countries that require copyright registration you would register your copyright.

2. You own copyright to something because you paid for it.

This is not true. The contract terms commissioning the work govern whether you will have copyright. If there is no written contract transferring ownership, copyright will automatically arise in favour of the creator rather than you, unless the creator is an employee on your payroll. The person paying for the work just has a licence to use it (and this licence is a lot narrower than the rights copyright ownership would give). In most countries worldwide, copyright will belong to the creator of a work unless there is a written agreement to the contrary. This is one reason why you should not commission an agency to develop your brand until you have a written contract with the agency detailing who is to have ownership of the assets created during the exercise.

3. **You need to register your copyright to secure protection to it.**

The Berne Convention and other international treaties ensure that copyright protection is secured internationally. If registration is not required in your home country, then you automatically get the benefit of copyright protection in all the countries that are signatories to these treaties – even in other countries where registration is a pre-requisite of protection. The one exception to this worth noting is that in the US any damages claims are subject to prior registration. To be on the safe side, then, some people do choose to register their copyright in the USA.

A pirate Christmas Carol

The reason why copyright is now the subject of international agreements is to protect creators from financial loss due to international piracy. Here is an example: when it was first published in 1843, Charles Dickens' famous story *A Christmas Carol* sold 6,000 copies. Yet Dickens made little money from the book. This is because, in Victorian times, copyright laws only protected a work inside the country in which it was first produced and created. After *A Christmas Carol* was published, copies started popping up abroad in America, produced by publishing houses very cheaply – and these pirated copies gave Dickens no financial benefit. Copyright is an important right that underpins the economic benefits in many industries – and now with international agreements in place, those economic benefits can be protected throughout most of the world.

4. Registering a trademark is optional.

A trademark acts as a sort of virtual container in which the brand value generated in the business is captured. Generally, this container is only effective if the trademark is capable of being registered as a word mark and is actually registered. Although it is possible to have unregistered trademark rights in some common law countries, unregistered rights are very weak and expensive to enforce and prove. It is prudent to secure the rights in assets, such as the name that underpins your brand, by registering a trademark. Registration makes it less expensive to enforce your rights and avoids the risk of someone else securing rights to the same name, causing you to have to rebrand. There will be more on trademarking in part 4, the naming section of the book. In the meantime, note that once you have registered a trademark you may use the R symbol ® to alert others that it is a registered trademark. Use of the TM symbol is totally meaningless because people often use it for names they would not be able to register.

5. Copyright protects the ideas underlying your writings.

Ideas, systems, or methods are not protected by copyright. What copyright protects is the *expression* of an idea, system, or method: in other words, the output. Copyright protects the *way an idea is expressed* rather than the idea itself. This is often referred to as the idea/expression dichotomy. For example, let us take a copyright work like a food recipe: the words of that specific recipe are protected by copyright. The ideas contained in the recipe are not. If someone sets your recipe out in their book, or copies and distributes it, they may well infringe your copyright. If they cook what is in your recipe, using the ideas in it, they do not. So, if it is a recipe for making apple pie, anyone can make apple pie to the recipe and sell the pies commercially, or they could vary the recipe and cook their own version of apple pie to make and sell or give away.

This also means that if you suggest an idea for someone else to execute, such as an unusual looking picture of a bird, or you give them an idea for a story they could write, the person creating the picture or writing the story would own copyright in the picture or plot produced. You as the person who came up with the ideas will have no copyright in the work created as a result of your ideas unless there is a legal agreement between you and the other party that states otherwise, or the creator is on your payroll. Ideas are not protected by copyright. The expression of ideas is.

6. **You can secure rights over an idea, method, or process by writing it down and having proof that it was your idea.**

If your idea is patentable, you need a patent to protect it from copyists – copyright is not sufficient to protect a patentable invention or idea. The law does not give rights to the person who first thinks of an idea, so writing down your ideas and depositing them along with drawings with a professional *does not give you rights to the idea*. Depositing material would at best help provide evidence that the work was created before the date it was deposited. This could be useful proof to establish the date of creation of a copyright work, but in the case of a patentable invention, process, or idea – it is pointless. The alternative to registering a patent is to keep the information confidential.

7. **Names are protected by copyright, or it is sufficient to register a company or secure the .com domain in order to be able to use a name.**

As a matter of policy, the law protects names through trademarks rather than through copyright. Regardless of how much investment or time is put into the creation of a name, no matter how clever it is, names are generally outside the scope of copyright protection. Trademarks are what give you exclusive rights to a name.

This means that you should only move on to have visual identity work carried out for you once you have secured the rights to the name on which the brand will be developed.

See chapter two as to why it is never enough to start using a name just because you secure the .com domain.

8. **You do not need to pick a unique brand name if your plan is to sell the business instead of growing it.**

The purpose of a name and its role in business is to enable a business to stand out for its products and services, and to protect the business against competitor actions that are quite likely if your business succeeds. Choosing a distinctive name that uniquely belongs to you and securing your ownership of it is the most basic step to capturing the value you create as you build the business. It should be regarded as part of the cost of doing business because the legal system protects businesses against threats that can and do arise in a connected global environment through the name. Using an inadequate name OR not securing rights to your unique brand identifier (that is, your name) is to overlook the most basic aspect of IP and branding. The name is not just about whether you want to use the same brand forever. It is a container of value. When a business is bought, the name may no longer be used, but your domain name will redirect to the business that now owns your former business. Sometimes they may add a note saying, 'now incorporating x'.

In the next chapter we will consider designing IP strategy into the creative process before the visual brand is produced. This involves prioritizing resources on building assets that can be owned immediately, even before they are uniquely associated with your brand, and protecting them from the outset.

Take home messages

- The main aspects of IP are patents, design rights, trademarks, copyright, and confidential information.
- Register trademarks to protect brand elements (including the name) that identify your business as the source of goods and services.
- Copyright protects the expression of an idea; it automatically arises in favour of the creator rather than you, unless the creator is an employee on your payroll or you have a written contract transferring ownership.
- Use a statutory declaration (UK) or registration to protect copyright ownership.
- Intellectual assets such as know-how, trade secrets, and ideas are only protected by IP law while they are kept *confidential*. If confidential information is stolen or leaked, the remedy is to bring a legal action against whoever misused that information.

CHAPTER 4

Think IP first!

In chapter 3, we became familiar with the concept of IP, and in chapter 2 we had a short introduction to the problems that can arise from ignoring IP in your branding process. In this chapter, we are going to look in more detail at the first step of the TUNED branding framework: think IP first.

The aim should be to create a distinctive brand that stands out in your category and looks unmistakeably like you. You should not be confused for a competitor. What is involved to do that?

Choosing IP assets as barriers to entry

Reaching customers is about creating brand assets that get their attention, help them to remember you, and make you recognizably different from competitors. The brand assets you prioritize creating should be protectable IP *and protected once created*, to deter copying and preserve your distinctiveness and commercial viability. IP is not a hurdle to jump. Rather, it is a useful tool in your business arsenal that helps you to decide what to create. This goes beyond doing clearance searches to check whether a proposed intangible element is available to use.

More than simply checking availability, think of IP as erecting 'barriers to entry', or as Warren Buffet refers to it: a moat around your business.[4] As well as identifying an advantage that your business might offer that is difficult to mimic or duplicate and thus creates an effective barrier against competition from others, you should aim to create distinctive branding that sets you apart and makes you more recognizable.

This is not as easy as it sounds, though: much copying that occurs in business is not legally actionable, and many of the distinctive assets you might use in business are not ownable except after long and prolonged use over time. Even then you may not be able to secure ownership of them. It makes sense, then, to prioritize creating and protecting assets you can readily own and place less emphasis on assets you are unlikely to ever own when building your brand.

Jenni Romaniuk, a professor conducting research at the Ehrenberg-Bass Institute and author of the book *Building Distinctive Brand Assets*, says (page 41) that branding 'is about making the brand name memorable – nothing more, but also nothing less'. She researched the extent to which various brand assets can substitute for the brand name once a brand becomes sufficiently well known.

The type of non-name signifiers that you might choose to build mental associations with your brand name might include:

1. A logo
2. A face icon – such as a symbol of an animal
3. A shape icon – such as McDonald's M, golden arches
4. The shape of packaging – such as the Coca-Cola bottle

---

[4] According to Investopedia, 'the term economic moat, popularized by Warren Buffett, refers to a business' ability to maintain competitive advantages over its competitors in order to protect its long-term profits and market share from competing firms': www.investopedia.com/ask/answers/05/economicmoat.asp

5. A distinctive font – such as the Snickers chocolate font
6. A tagline phrase – such as Just Do It.
7. A sound – such as the 118 118 jingle or music that is associated with the brand
8. A colour or group of colours – such as the Tiffany blue
9. A celebrity endorser
10. Design of a product or its packaging
11. A look and feel that is protected – such as of a website or the internal layout of the Apple Store
12. Photographs, illustrations, and imagery
13. Content created on a website, or copy used in the ad and in any scripts created for an ad or video – such as the Marks and Spencer ads that say 'This is not just food… This is M&S food'

IP laws apply to these assets in different ways, meaning there are different actions you need to take to secure your rights depending on what you choose to create. Different considerations arise when deciding whether to use an asset because the steps involved to protect an asset depend on what the asset is. Protection is how the asset remains unique to your brand and enables you to take effective action should competitors copy you. Protection of some assets, such as celebrity endorsements, focuses on the legal agreement you use with the celebrity; while for others, such as music, the key is both the legal agreement *and* applying for available IP registrations. In the case of music, this would be the agreements when licensing use or commissioning a piece of music to be written for you; and either copyright ownership or trademarking, or both.

To reach a stage where people automatically associate a distinctive element of your brand with your brand name takes time, and repeated and consistent use. Legal protection is key in giving you the time and space to build those associations to your brand in buyers' memories while keeping competitors at bay. Place less emphasis initially on those assets you are unlikely to ever own as you build your brand. Instead focus on some basic assets you can readily own. Then in due course, once you have built these initial assets, you might choose others to associate to your brand. Consider the legal dimension before choosing promotional or creative designs.

Your brand name and key brand assets can provide patent-like protection for your successful business *provided they are well chosen and are properly protected and enforced*.

Incidentally, if you don't yet have the financial resources to put into branding, or just want to test your ideas quickly, I suggest adopting a temporary name (even if there is a name you really want to use), and use low-cost visual designs while you test your business idea. This means you can get started and get market feedback for your business idea quickly and cost effectively. Then with greater insight into your market, choose a suitable name and visual identity. As mentioned in chapter 9, many well-known brands started out with a different identity initially.

Uniqueness and fame

In her book, Romaniuk identifies two drivers of brand asset strength: uniqueness and fame. For example, when you see the swoosh logo of the Nike brand, you know it represents Nike even though it may be featured on its own with no name accompanying it. Nike has been using the swoosh logo since the mid-1970s, and until the swoosh became famous on its own, it would have been accompanied by the brand name. The Nike swoosh is *unique* in its category (that means, no competitors were using a similar icon), and it is also *famous* because the asset is recognized and linked to the Nike brand by most people. If an asset is less famous, it is more likely to be mistakenly attributed to a competitor's brand.

To see more examples of non-name signifiers that you might choose to build mental associations to your brand, including design trademark examples of different brand elements, check out the brandtuned.com/blog. The design trademark examples category covers the examples in this chapter more visually as well as discussing the considerations to bear in mind if you are choosing less inherently distinctive symbols, such as the Adidas three-stripes.

When the mere use of a visual like your symbol acquires the power to bring your brand to mind you have a distinctive shortcut to trigger memories in buyers' minds. This protects your underlying business because the trust that the market has in Nike goods is remembered just by virtue of the swoosh logo. The logo motivates consumers to buy the brand's products.

A distinctive asset such as the Nike swoosh would have been capable of being owned as a trademark as soon as the design was completed. This means Nike would have been able to register it as a trademark immediately and could have readily stopped competitors using the swoosh logo *or any similar design* to promote the type of goods Nike sells under that brand.

It goes without saying that if you can secure a trademark over a distinctive asset immediately, then you should do so

– because that is how you maintain its uniqueness and ensure you can be associated with that element over time. Securing legal protection gives you scope to build associations to your brand name with that brand asset, so it forms part of your distinctive identity. Your advertising budget could be tiny, but you can still confidently build up recognition to such an asset because if you have protected it, you have powerful rights available to you to fend off copyists. However, if you cannot legally protect an asset immediately, then it is much more difficult to build up unique associations to that asset for your brand. You would just have to hope that a competitor did not adopt a similar brand asset that confused buyers as to who was behind the brand.

It makes sense therefore, before creating brand assets, to look at competitors in your category to decide how to stand out in relation to them. While you want to avoid blending in with what everyone else is doing – for example, if everyone is using a certain type of sans serif font because it is the fashion to have a clean uncluttered look, it is probably a bad idea to follow suit – there are some parameters that you might need to adopt to fit with the category. Here is a simple example: if you decide to be different to all the other milk brands by putting your milk in black bottles, then buyers may not notice your brand because they are not expecting to see milk in black bottles. So, whatever you do to stand out as a milk brand should probably include using white or cream as a background colour, and respecting the standard colourings used in the industry to denote whether the milk is skimmed, semi-skimmed etc. Beyond that you are free to brand through your use of a unique name, and visual designs such as a distinctive symbol, font, a striking accent colour, a clever tagline, and so on. First stocktake to see what your competitors are doing, and then choose three or four elements to create a visual identity that sets your brand apart from theirs so you are unique-looking and distinctive. What you choose to create is impacted by IP law, and you also need to protect those assets immediately – that is how you create a distinctive brand that stands the test of time.

Coca-Cola was driven to create its iconic bottle to fend off copying. Competitor brands were copying the company using names like Koka-Nola, Ma Coca-Co, Toka-Cola, and even Koke. They copied or only slightly modified the font of its logo, and their bottles created confusion among consumers, many of whom were illiterate. While Coca-Cola litigated against these copyists, the cases took years to produce results. Developing its unique bottle shape was the company's answer to help even illiterate customers to distinguish the brand from its imitators. This tactic reduced the effectiveness of copycats.

Case study: Coca-Cola

Coca-Cola was able to secure trademark ownership of its iconic bottle shape by firstly having the right legal agreement in place when it commissioned the bottle design. Secondly, they made strategic use of the available IP protections to protect the design of the bottle shape against copying once they began to use it.

This initial protection of the design meant that certain types of copying by competitors could be legally challenged. Coca-Cola then gradually associated its bottle shape in consumers' minds with its brand by using clever advertising that consistently featured the bottle shape. Getting trademark rights over shapes is not easy. It is necessary to provide evidence that the shape is uniquely associated with your brand. After some 14 years the shape became synonymous with the Coca-Cola brand. That is when the company knew that the shape was a symbol of its brand, meaning they could confidently apply to register it as a trademark.

By taking full advantage of the legal protections that the law offers, and knowing how to focus resources, Coca-Cola was able to get this powerful protection. While design rights over a shape only last a finite period, a trademark lasts for as long as you use it and renew your trademark registration. Potentially Coca-Cola will have this monopoly right over its distinctive bottle shape forever provided it makes use of the bottle and keeps evidence of its use in case any competitor challenges its rights and applies to cancel its registration.

It follows from the Coca-Cola example that you can make informed decisions about which assets to create and build for your brand – considering your available budget and resources. With some assets, like Coca-Cola's bottle shape, you need to use them consistently and invest a substantial marketing and advertising budget over a substantial period before you can stand a chance of owning them as your trademark. The ideal is to have some protection in the interim to justify the investment in building an asset.

Colour marks

Many people think of brand colours as an important primary decision for their visual identity, but colour should be a secondary consideration for many businesses because colour marks require a very substantial marketing and advertising budget, over many years, to secure. So, while you should use your brand colours consistently, you do need to accept that you will be largely powerless to stop competitors who use similar colours. In theory in countries like the UK you may be able to initiate a passing off action against competitors who use similar colours, but in practice passing off is likely to have limited use for most businesses.

Household-name brands that have achieved colour trademark registrations include Tiffany's turquoise, 3M's yellow, Coca-Cola's red, UPS' brown, and Barbie's pink. However, the bar to registration of a colour trademark is high. The brands that succeed in securing a colour trademark need to first become associated with a colour. In other words, you need to be able to prove that the colour has a secondary meaning unique to your brand's goods or services. Secondary meaning is shown by a high volume of advertising involving the colour mark, as well as consumer surveys establishing that a high degree of relevant consumers associate that colour or combination with your brand.

However, the difficulty with colour marks is that there is no real interim legal protection available to rely on as you build up recognition for the asset. This means you need a strategy to use colour in appropriate ways if your aim is to secure trademark protection. Apart from that, you need to rely purely on your substantial marketing and advertising budget to promote a colour asset. If competitors use the same elements – the same colour, for example – it may create confusion as to which brand is the source of that asset. In other words, consumers will not be able to tell whether the colour is being used by you, or by a competing brand.

This means that, in practice, there is a constant interplay between use and ownership. If brand confusion is created and you have legal rights over the brand element, then you should enforce your rights to prevent the market confusion from continuing. On the other hand, if you do not own the asset, you may decide to just stop using it to avoid buyers confusing you with your competition – especially if the competitor has greater brand recognition in that element, such as in that colour. You may especially want to consider changing a colour you are using if:

- the colour is the same as a competitor's colour,
- brand confusion is becoming evident,
- you do not have legal protection for the colour yet, and
- the competitor has a greater marketing budget than you.

This is because, as we have said, it requires a substantial marketing budget and a dedicated long-term strategy to stand a chance of securing legal protection of a colour asset.

On the other hand, if you have the bigger budget, that could be to your advantage. Having high spending power acts as a disincentive to competitors copying the same colour during that risky period while you are building up recognition for that colour asset – even though legal steps may not be available to protect the colour in the interim. Your high spending on advertising means competitors would risk misattribution to your brand if they began using that colour. They would not want to spend their marketing budget on promoting your brand.

Here is an example of colour trademarking not being done well or successfully. General Mills' bid to register the yellow colour of its Cheerios cereal boxes in 2017 failed, even though the company had used that colour since 1945, because yellow was already widely used in the category. From their example, we can see that, in addition to the above, standing a chance of establishing secondary meaning involves choosing colours, or a combination of colours, that are not already widely used within your target market. Given that the colour yellow was widely used in the category, General Mills' strategy should have been to change its colour in some way and rely on becoming known for its distinctive use of a colour in its category.

Remember: a strong brand asset needs both fame *and* uniqueness – which is much harder to achieve with a colour!

What is in a name?

Trying to secure ownership of a colour that is in standard use in a category, such as in the General Mills example, is like trying to secure a generic name or common word as a trademark – something people seem to want to do in their quest to find meaning in the names they choose. But that is not what branding is designed to do. Even if you did secure protection of an industry term or colour, you would find it very expensive to enforce your rights and would become extremely unpopular in the process too – because competitors need to be able to use the generic descriptors that you are trying to monopolize. Ultimately, one of them would almost certainly challenge your registration by applying to have it cancelled, which would be a long and expensive process to defend and may not be successful anyway.

We will look more at choosing the right name in part 4.

Mental availability

Coming back to Romaniuk's two principles of uniqueness and fame, trademarks are about creating something unique and distinctive to you, and then protecting that uniqueness so it can become famously associated with your brand. The interesting part, from my perspective as an IP lawyer, is that Romaniuk's analysis suggests that the assets most likely to meet this double criterion of uniqueness and fame are also the ones that you can readily protect from day one, such as the Nike swoosh. In other words, her study sheds light on the importance of legal protection for acquiring recognition of your distinctive brand assets.

Let us look at this in more detail: your brand assets need to be distinctive so buyers can immediately *find* and *recognize* you when they are looking to buy the products and services you sell. As well as standing out by looking distinctive, you should focus on ensuring you are present wherever buyers look to buy your category.

The first task a brand has is to raise awareness of its existence. Once people know it exists, those people need to mentally link your brand name to the type of products or services you sell.

Let us take this book as an example. If my brand is called Brand Tuned, I need people first to know the name Brand Tuned so it is a thing that exists within their consciousness, and then I need people to know what Brand Tuned offers: brand and IP consultancy – that is brand coaching, mentoring, and education that integrates brand creation with brand protection. Once people have associated the brand name with the products or services of the brand, the brand is said to have 'mental availability' (also called brand salience or awareness).

Having mental availability is the first crucial step towards being chosen in a buying situation and standing a chance to come to mind for buyers when they are ready to spend money on the type of products and services you sell. What this means, if I've understood the Ehrenberg-Bass Institute's ideas correctly, is that when a buyer is ready to buy the type of product or service your brand sells, there should be a connection with your brand in their minds. When they think of that type of product or service – you want them to also think of your brand. It is not enough to be the other way round, that your brand creates a connection with that thing; that is the wrong way round. For example, if I want Brand Tuned to be thought about by buyers when they are thinking about branding and how to develop or define their brand, that means phrases like 'IP and branding', 'brand management', and 'brand identity and IP mentoring' need to bring Brand Tuned to mind. It is not enough for Brand Tuned to make people think of branding and IP, brand identity brand management, or mentoring, etc. Burger King may make you think of burgers – but if when you think of burgers, McDonald's comes to mind, then the brand association is not strong enough for a buyer to choose Burger King.

So how do you achieve this connection in your target customers? The starting point is to understand your market, and what buyers are thinking about when looking for a solution from your category, so you can build up associations to your brand in your advertising and promotional activities. The concept of 'category entry points' is a way of talking about the reasons or occasions when buyers consider buying a product or service from your category, and it is key to increasing your brand's mental availability for each buying situation. Find out when and where the buyer is looking to buy the category, as well as who they are with or who is advising them, and whether they are buying something else alongside the category – and you will be one step closer to creating the right content to enable them to notice your brand amongst all the others in your category. I discuss building mental availability more in chapter 12 of this book.

A known brand – in the above example, it would be Brand Tuned if it became known – becomes a node in someone's memory, along with other linked attributes and associations. To access our memories, we need a point of entry or *cue*. For a memory of your grandma, this might mean getting a whiff of her perfume, while for a brand association, the cue will be a category entry point. Distinctive brand assets will sit in the brand's network of associations. The ideal is for those assets not to have rich, multi-layered, or complex meaning says Romaniuk, because then other meanings that are not unique to the brand could potentially divert the buyer's attention away. Ideally, you want your brand assets to have simple meanings that remind the buyer only of your brand. The more category entry points your brand is attached to, the greater the number of retrieval pathways available to your brand.

All of this means that your marketing strategy to bring your brand to buyers' attention would do well to focus on a goal of broadening the brand's category entry point network rather than trying to own a single attribute, according to Byron Sharp and Jenni Romaniuk. This is a very different approach to what is generally believed to be the way to brand a business, and it is an area of controversy in the branding industry currently.

There are three purposes to using brand assets:

- **Ownership** – to denote the origin of products or services as emanating from a source who is known for delivering a particular promise to customers.

- **Anchor** – to anchor the brand in the customer's mind. For example, you will recognize McDonald's and the golden arches as brand assets already. Then if you see a promotion of McCafe, that associates coffee with your original memories of these assets so that the McDonald's brand will be recalled when you are next looking to buy coffee.
- **Bridge** – to act as a bridge between different marketing activities.

Daniel Kahneman, who wrote the book *Thinking, Fast and Slow* (2012), explains how our brains are wired to use two modes of thought: system 1, which is fast, instinctive, and emotional; and system 2, which is slower, more effortful, logical, and deliberate. The two modes complement each other. We need to bear this in mind when we take any actions designed to persuade or influence others, such as when selecting the intangible assets to create for our brand, or in promotional campaigns. Decision science tells us that most of our daily decisions are made automatically and unconsciously using our system 1. We use our more logical system 2 for decisions that we consciously need to make, but this is a limited resource that is easily depleted as we get tired. As humans, we are naturally wired to make less use of system 2 thinking when making decisions such as which brands to buy. Whenever you are creating or re-designing a brand, keep in mind this way that humans process the world around them.

In addition to knowing that many of our consumers' decisions to buy from us may well be subconscious, Byron Sharp's *How Brands Grow* found that many of our existing preconceptions about brands and branding are wrong. In particular, he shoots down the widespread misconception that loyalty is the metric to try to create, pointing out that the user profiles of brands are the same. In other words, your buyers are no different to your competitors' buyers. You share the same customers. The implication of Sharp's ideas is that branding is terribly important – not for building deep emotional connections with consumers, as is generally thought, but in the *battle for attention*. Consumers are very busy with other things, which is why Sharp emphasizes how misguided it is to assume they fall in love with brands. However, even heavy category buyers do not buy all the brands that are on the market; they keep returning to some favourites.

So, if you cannot rely on 'customer loyalty' and you can't necessarily rely on being able to capture your customers' 'system 2' thinking – why do these buyers come back to their favourite brands? Often, it is to simplify their lives to make choices effortlessly. To be able to return to a favourite brand, they must *recognize* the brand and *notice* it, which means the brand must be *present* wherever they are looking to buy.

Brand discovery and recognition, and IP

The most effective aim of your branding activities, then, will be to focus on helping buyers to *find* and *recognize* you. We want to create the situation that when they are looking to buy, your brand comes to their attention, and that they can readily find you again if they have previously come across your brand. We cannot rely on all our customers remembering that we exist. Even if buyers want to find you, they may have an imperfect memory of your identity. If a potential buyer noticed you or even bought you a while back and is now looking to buy the type of product or service you sell, you need to come to their consideration set. The buyer will be in system 1 mode. The job of your brand is to come to the buyer's attention again or to be noticed for the first time if they have never come across you before. It could be your brand name, logo, tagline, or symbol that jogs the buyer's memory and reminds them of your existence. This is where branding and IP need to work together. Whatever it is about your branding that triggers a customer's memory or gets their attention should be distinctive and legally owned by you ideally.

The brand name is the anchor that identifies you, although it may be your distinctive logo, font, tagline, or other imagery that attracts the buyer's attention. It will not always be the same brand element that lodges itself in a buyer's memory and jogs them into noticing your brand. IP laws, if properly used, serve to ensure you remain distinctively recognizable because, although competitors will copy your business model and approach to solving problems so that you may be indistinguishable from each other eventually, if you have chosen your brand assets carefully and protected and enforced them, competitors will not be able to copy your distinctive brand assets. If you think about IP first – *before* creating your brand identity – you will be better placed to choose what to create to achieve a distinctive stand-out brand. IP helps you to know which three to four brand elements would be optimal to prioritize so you can ensure your brand can be uniquely recognizable in the busy lives of potential buyers. Protecting those assets is part and parcel of ensuring that what you create remains unique to you and is not copied. And then do not change your core brand elements.

Leaving IP until after the name and brand assets are already chosen opens you up to some of the problems that we have seen in the previous chapters as well as to others, some of which we will see in this chapter and the naming section of the book. The best strategy is to get advice about IP for your brand before you embark on a visual design exercise as well as during the exercise. At its most basic, making choices of brand elements should take into account how protectable your choices are, quite apart from whether the elements are legally available and suitable for your business objectives. I will explain this by using my own brand as an example.

My branding journey

Back in 2014, I read a great branding book, called *Visual Hammer: Nail your Brand into the Mind with the Emotional Power of a Visual* by Laura Ries (2012). The main concept from Ries' book that stuck with me was the one from the title – the idea of a 'visual hammer' to knock home your brand into people's minds. She argued that every consumer has two sides to their brain: one verbal and one visual. The aim of successful branding is to bring both sides of the brain together in your visual identity. At the time, I had a typographic logo for Azrights, and inspired by this idea of a 'visual hammer' I decided to incorporate the image of a bull to denote the original concept of branding (branding cattle). Brand protection was the focus of our IP services hence the choice of a bull to drive this home with a visual hammer. We also had a new tagline, which I wanted to incorporate into our visual identity as well. But in trying to shoehorn all those things together, now the branding was looking a mess. This is what it looked like:

The visual brand had evolved in a somewhat haphazard way since the original logo was designed for us in 2006. So, I was open to the idea of having a brand refresh when a designer I knew approached me to suggest this. I had just written my book *Legally Branded* and introduced various new products in the business, so it seemed a good time. However, what I ended up with after the 'brand refresh' was a new logo, no visual hammer, and a new tagline to reflect an aspect of our positioning, namely that we work with tech companies and online brands. Here is the logo I ended up with:

Back in 2014, I did not realize that distinctive brand assets might have recognition value, so it seemed no big deal to accept changes to the colours, font, and tagline. I had assumed that a brand refresh would give me a more aesthetically pleasing way of combining the various existing brand assets; I had not envisaged that everything would change. Back then I did not know as much as I now know about branding and assumed there were intrinsic reasons why my visual identity needed to change and could not incorporate a visual hammer. I accepted the situation the designer presented me with. I liked the new logo well enough, so what is the problem? The fact that our old branding was discarded and that the new brand made no use of the bull or our easy legal tagline (which was a registered trademark) is not so much a reflection on this designer as it is of the branding industry. It is not uncommon for designers to start all over again rather than building on what is already there.

Now, this is not a disaster story: to be honest, I doubt that, at the time, any of the Azrights brand assets had built up enough recognition for it to matter. After all, I had only used the bull icon for about a year. However, when a change happens for more well-known brands, even a less radical change can have damaging consequences. Romaniuk cites the example of Tropicana. A juice company, primarily known for orange juice, they went for a redesigned visual to position themselves as a more premium brand, which resulted in the oranges on their boxes being dropped. While this certainly created a more upmarket look, it also resulted in the loss of a ton of sales. In that case the design team had done some research before changing the branding, but their research had focused on the wrong questions – instead of establishing how famous and unique the oranges on the packaging were, they had focused on whether the absence of the oranges gave the packaging a more premium look.

Whenever you change an asset, what you disrupt are the buyers' memory structures that you had previously worked so hard to build. By considering how buyers think of and notice the category or buy your brand, and how brands fit into their lives, it is much more possible to make branding decisions and run campaigns that guide buyers to think of your brand in different contexts and situations. Being in system 1 mode, as we all tend to be when looking for products and services to buy, we may well not notice a brand we have previously used if its visual identity changes.

So, back to my branding journey. In 2020, around the time I was planning this book, I was ready to make some more changes. My business was going through a transition; for one thing, I was planning on introducing Brand Tuned. So, the time seemed right to tweak the Azrights brand. I hoped to get that visual hammer in place that I had wanted since reading Laura Ries' book in 2014.

I found a designer who agreed to help create a distinctive symbol icon to fit with the existing Azrights logo. However, as soon as I had signed up to use his services, I realized this might not be the right person for my brand to work with because he announced that it was a bad idea to tack on new elements to existing brand designs and to just tweak those base designs. Instead, he wanted to create a completely new brand, new logo, new fonts, new colouring, the lot. The first designer had not been able to give me a symbol when she had a complete clean slate, and now here was this new designer telling me to rebrand to add a symbol icon! Still, we persevered… one of the things we tried was using a sextant, a navigation instrument for measuring distances between objects, as a symbol. I feared it might only have worked with a new Azrights logo using a capital A and would therefore have required a completely new logo design. However, a bigger problem was that when we did an availability search on the sextant logo, we found an Italian law firm that was using a sextant in their logo and that had called themselves Sextant. They had registered their trademark.

Whenever availability searches throw up an issue like this, you need to consider your appetite for risk. You can decide to accept the risk and maybe set aside a contingency budget for litigation, or you can avoid a dispute by choosing a different asset.

An example of how disputes over similar icons can play out is provided in a case involving Jack Wills Limited and the House of Fraser stores in 2014. The so called 'Mr Wills' logo featured a pheasant wearing a top hat and tailcoat, holding a cane. The House of Fraser logo featured a pigeon wearing a top hat and tailcoat, and a bow tie. The court decided that House of Fraser had infringed the Mr Wills trademark and ordered House of Fraser to account for its profits from sales of the clothing featuring the logo. This case provides an example of why it is important to consider IP first before creating an asset. See trademark examples at brandtuned.com/blog.

So, we decided no-go on the sextant. At this point, I decided to call it a day with this designer – he was very good but was the wrong fit for my branding needs at the time. Given the knowledge I had gathered over the years about branding – to the point where I was about to start writing a book on branding! – I decided to take on the work myself, with the help of a couple of talented graphic designers who helped us with design services. I remembered the bull icon we had previously used and that we had chosen it to denote branding. It was the reason the cover of my book *Legally Branded* uses cattle too. I hit on the idea of a ram as an icon to signify branding because I thought this might fit with our existing lower case logo. Rams reflect strength and the power to overcome and to achieve breakthroughs. They denote action, the fifth element of heroism. When you bear in mind that I am an Aries, the star sign that is associated with a ram, it seemed a perfect fit to use a ram as the basis of our icon.

The designers did a great job. This is the ram icon and altered logo I ended up with.

It fitted with the existing Azrights logo (which we tweaked), and I decided to make a few other adjustments to the colours, and to reinstate our trademarked tagline because 'lawyers for the digital world' was bound to date, whereas 'easy legal not legalese' incorporates a value of ours around the use of plain English and providing accessible information on the law. I kept the colour fade idea from my previous logo. This time, I had learned my lesson about retaining memory-triggering features.

And importantly – the ram posed no conflicts with any existing logo registrations by law firms or branding agencies. I finally had a visual hammer that was unique and held the potential to gather recognition for the Azrights brand!

When it came to creating a complementary icon for Brand Tuned, the other part of my business, I did not try to find a meaningful symbol as I had with the ram. The Ehrenberg-Bass Institute point out that your brand symbols need not be meaningful, because what really counts is distinctiveness. So, I opted for a meaningless-but-stand-out owl. There was no other rationale for it!

Branding is in a state of flux

I have used my own business as a case study to demonstrate the difficulty of building distinctive assets gradually. Some designers are quick to suggest a new logo, or to want to change everything – this is understandable, as visual creativity is what they are paid for! But it is only a part of what makes up successful branding. Good design matters, but so does recognition and memorability. This must be a primary consideration, and IP must be borne in mind first when deciding what to create and protect. Learn from my experience: rather than trying to tack on a symbol or other icon later, make sure that, if you want one, your visual identity comes with one from the outset.

At the time of writing, the world of branding is in a state of flux. We have old, possibly outdated, notions of what it takes to create a brand, and a new body of knowledge from the Ehrenberg-Bass research. It is a difficult time to know to whom to entrust your branding projects. In my case, I have learned that to get the best outcome for my brand, I need to stay involved and not to hand over wholesale to a designer. Taking care to select the right person to work with is key. Maybe your creative process will be different, but to end up with the right branding you need to have some ideas yourself about what you want. Think through your brand without involving a designer initially, and only engage someone once you have developed your ideas more fully. You will then be better placed to choose the right creative to work with.

And use what you have learned in this section. The brand assets you use need to make life *easier* for buyers. They have intrinsic value – so do not just throw away something that you have been using. It may have built up some recognition. Once you have chosen something new, you could lose business if your potential customers cannot recognize you by the familiar signs they know. Measure the fame and uniqueness of your existing assets before discarding them.

Your brand guidelines should focus on how to use your brand assets consistently across media and in ads to get mental recognition in the different contexts in which any new assets will be used, focusing on how the assets will work together as a whole. They provide mental shortcuts and act as a quick reminder of the brand; ad campaigns should therefore carefully consider use of brand elements so someone who saw the last campaign can recognize this one as emanating from the same source. Remember buyers are often in system 1 mode coming across hundreds of brands in a single day.

Law is the framework for how society operates in different areas of activity, and IP laws play an important role in branding. Acquiring uniqueness and fame of assets involves taking account of IP early on rather than treating IP as a separate activity to engage with optionally after the brand is created.

Designing IP strategy into the creative process before the visual brand is created is about prioritizing building assets that can be owned immediately, even before they are uniquely associated with your brand. I suggest allocating a budget to protecting them as part of your branding budget. Protection is key to preserving the distinctiveness that visual designs produce. There is no point spending thousands on a visual identity and leaving nothing in the pot to protect those assets.

Take home messages

- Create a distinctive brand that stands out in your category and looks unmistakably like you.
- Use non-name signifiers to build mental associations with your brand name (e.g. a logo, distinctive font, tagline phrase, or packaging design). Begin with basic assets you can readily own.
- Think through your brand and get advice about IP before involving a designer.
- Understand your market so you can build up associations with your brand in your advertising and promotional activities, focusing on helping buyers to find and recognize you.
- Create brand guidelines to use your brand assets consistently across media and in ads to get mental recognition in different contexts.

Part 2

t u n e d

Understand the market

In this part, we will explore the importance of understanding your market – as well as understanding yourself and your motivations for creating a brand, and then looking at competitors, customers, and how to position your business in that context.

CHAPTER 5

Business strategy

Now that you have a better understanding of how IP relates to branding, the next step in your journey is to understand the market to determine your business strategy.

Whether you are embarking on a new business, or rethinking an existing business, the starting point is to consider what you want to achieve with the business, what your hopes and aspirations for it are, and then decide how to develop your ideas and brand. Testing the concept will be key, depending on what it is you are introducing to the market.

Once you are ready to launch the business fully, you need a business plan. Just as you would not build a house without a plan, so it is unwise to embark on a business without forethought. It need not be a lengthy plan, but it is important to have one, and to revisit and update it at least annually. Clarity about the problem you solve, which customers you solve it for, and what your stance will be helps you approach the problem you are solving more effectively.[5]

Some people put insufficient thought into their business and launch without a clear plan. Instead of thinking about the substance of what their brand is to deliver they move straight to getting a visual identity because they want measurable, tangible things for their money and assume that a visual identity exercise

---

[5] Oliver Gassmann, Karolin Frankenberger, and Michaela Csik, *The Business Model Navigator* (2014).

will give them all they need to get going with their business. So, they are often answering questions covered in this part 2 of the book for the first time during their visual design work. It is inappropriate to expect creatives to hand-hold you to understand your vision for your business. Their job is the creative stuff, not the business identity. The business identity is the job of the founders.

Design briefs can often be subject to misunderstanding, with designers and their clients not quite meeting in the middle, for whatever reason. As the client, you can avoid this by making sure you are able to clearly communicate your vision and ask the right questions to understand what the designer (or other creative) will and will not be able to do for you. To this end, thinking through your business strategy should come well before the brand strategy and visual design stage. As a bonus, it works out much cheaper in the long run to use designers at the end of the process rather than at the start of it, just as it works out much cheaper to think of IP at the start rather than leaving it till after a brand has already been created.

Thinking strategically

You need a three- to five-year business strategy with IP strategy as an important part of it. You will also need a brand strategy, as well as annual marketing and campaign strategies to build the brand and attract sales. Your brand strategy will draw from the business strategy while the marketing strategy will draw from both.

Ultimately, the goal of strategy is to identify the way to build a sustainable advantage over the competition. The business model is one of the ways of doing this. Think about your business vision, and the customers for whom you solve problems. By focusing on the end goals, and how you hope to achieve them, you will have clear answers when you turn to having your visual identity designed rather than thinking about them for the first time then.

While it is exciting to see your ideas transformed into appealing visual designs, hold off from changing the visual identity immediately you decide to create a brand or to rebrand an existing one. Even I had to stop myself looking for a designer as soon as I came up with the idea of Brand Tuned. Instead, I realized there was no hurry to think about visual designs. I would experiment, talk to potential customers, and work out the strategy before worrying about getting the right visual designs in place.

Success does not come from having an awesome looking logo or website, or a good name. It primarily involves *making better decisions*, often by virtue of having the right business model and strategy. The importance of thinking and planning should not be underestimated in business.

Business planning and business strategy

While it goes beyond the scope of this book to discuss how to write a business plan, it is a key activity to undertake as you think through your business. It is a valuable exercise in and of itself to give you clarity. Depending on the business idea, much of your proof-of-concept activities may be spent on visiting different elements of the business plan. If you need investment, your business plan has another purpose as well – in this case, it should be more formal and thorough to win over investors. Essentially, the exercise benefits you simply because you take the time to plan. It gives you a roadmap for better decision-making that you can return to and take stock of or update periodically. There are a host of issues your business plan will address, which is why business plans are outside the scope of this book. I want to emphasize the importance of the right business model in determining success. Think: easyJet versus British Airways, Dell versus HP, or Amazon versus Barnes & Noble.

Your business strategy is the high-level plan for reaching specific business objectives. The choice of objective is the heart of strategy. Consider the Innocent smoothie's brand: this grew faster than its main competitors, despite being higher in price. According to JN Kapferer,[6] Innocent was growing by 91%, Pete & Johnny's (PJ's) by 10%, and private labels by 24%.

Yet Innocent did not create this market. It came second. A brand called PJ's was the first mover in 1994. Innocent came in 1998. The key to Innocent's success was its strategy of promoting a healthy drink by sparking a debate between bad food and good food, between industry practices that focused on reducing costs and those that focused on what is good for consumers. Its choice of name, Innocent, that is, not guilty, was an important element of the brand. Having a strong point of view is possibly why it prevailed over PJ's, which was just a marketing brand trying to emulate the success of Ben & Jerry's. Innocent was a brand targeted at youth, a promise (health), and a brand personality (fun). However, PJ's had no authenticity, no real brand content, no true story, and no capacity to execute the promise without compromise at any cost – only a lot of money, as it was backed by PepsiCo.

---

[6] *The New Strategic Brand Management: Advanced Insights and Strategic Thinking* (2012).

Setting a vision for the future direction of the business helps you answer some of the fundamental questions that will form key components of your overall strategy.

A strategy is a way through a difficulty, an approach to overcoming an obstacle, a response to a challenge. If the challenge is not defined, it is difficult or impossible to assess the quality of the strategy. Richard Rumelt, author of *Good Strategy/Bad Strategy: The Difference and Why It Matters* (2017), suggests that the kernel of a strategy contains three elements:

1. a diagnosis,
2. a guiding policy, and
3. coherent action.

He warns against statements of desire that do not amount to a plan for overcoming obstacles.

Rumelt is also quite damning about what he classes as a 'templated approach' to deciding your vision, mission, and values. However, this approach to deciding business strategy has widespread favour in the SME market, and is a useful starting point to describe what your business does, what you plan to sell or offer, why, and to whom. It gives you a helicopter view of the issues and as such helps you take in what is happening – so it is what we are going to look at in this chapter, too.

There is no recipe for success

Rumelt is not alone in his disdain for cookie-cutter business. Phil Rosenzweig, in his book *The Halo Effect* (2007), counsels business managers to adopt a critical considered approach to strategy, rather than seeking a definitive recipe for success. He cites nine ways in which people fall into the trap of taking specific actions based on general impressions – the halo effect.

In the same vein, an excellent resource that was a real eye opener for me and is helpful for guiding your business thinking is the book *Beyond Strategy: The Impact of Next Generation Companies*. The authors, Michael Moesgaard Andersen and Flemming Poulfelt, convincingly demonstrate that no generic recipe for success exists in business. They explain that although some well-known leadership books suggest there is a recipe for success, the recipe in fact changes depending on the situation that a given company finds itself in. Different measures must be used for different circumstances.

The authors suggest regarding classic books on leadership and business as useful food for thought and good pointers on how to develop your business, and to not lose sight of the fact that a cookbook approach to business does not give you success. I hope this is how you will use *Brand Tuned*, too.

Vision

It is important to have a clear vision for your business.

As part of your search for determining what your vision should be, the simple act of writing down a list of the most important steps you think you need to take to achieve your objectives, picking one to go with (as an exercise), and setting a plan around achieving it can provide an invaluable way to start off your thinking. This helps you to take stock of where you are, so you can then decide what to do and how to focus resources based on which objective is truly important to you. Once you have chosen your goal your tactics will follow on; they are the steps you will take towards your goal.

As you do this thinking work, you will get a clearer picture of your vision for your business. Essentially, your vision is focused on the business you are creating and your reason for doing so. A combination of that vision and your values determines how you will design the business to support how you want it to be known, what you stand for, and what promise you want to deliver.

Amazon's vision is to be Earth's most customer-centric company, where customers can find and discover anything they might want to buy online.

Elon Musk's ambition is to move humanity forward in new directions. Tesla is essentially one of the vehicles he uses to achieve that goal.

How would you define your vision for your business to your-self, to your team, and to external audiences? How will they know what your business is all about?

What you stand for and believe in are the most essential elements of your brand. For many founders it will be something bigger than profit, and likely transcends the current business. Their stance is what enables them to build the right culture to support what they stand for as a business. An essential aspect of working out your purpose is to be very clear about your values because everything you do needs to align with them. I will come back to purpose later, but first let us consider your values.

Values

Values, in a vacuum, make little sense. You likely have numerous values that guide your life. You need to be selective when identifying your core values for your business – ideally you would be able to choose just three values. The question of which values you select therefore needs context: namely, what are your values about the type of products or services in your category? If you offer personal care products, then what are your values about personal care? If you provide legal services, what are your values around legal services? The values you select should be chosen by reference to who you are and what problem you want to solve in the business you are embarking on. For example, when I founded Azrights, one of my top values was to communicate in plain English. When I come across a lawyer who drafts in plain English and whose legal agreements are easy to understand, I feel they would represent the Azrights brand well. The report from the Brand Tuned scorecard test (www.brandtuned.com/scorecard) provides insight on how to think through your values.

The research you do to understand your market should help in uncovering some of the problems that exist in the category. By considering the category issues, decide what problems you want to focus on solving, and what you stand for. Think about what you like and dislike about the category.

Deciding what your values are impacts every other decision, including your positioning and brand promise, as well as the team you recruit. The behaviours your team need to adopt and display to consistently deliver the promise require sufficient clarity about your values so you can better communicate with everybody inside and outside the organization. Your values also impact the approach you take to the products and services you offer. If you do not create a culture where your values are aligned

towards your purpose as an organization, it is much more difficult to lead the business in the direction you want to take it.

Think about what deep beliefs you cherish above all else.
What your overarching ethos or values are, by which you want
to approach everything you do in your business. Your values
determine what you will and will not offer, where you play, what
you stand for. For example, in 2009 Tim Cook was asked about
Apple's strategy towards the booming Netbook market, where
many PC companies were introducing low-cost sub-notebooks
and chasing low-margin sales. Cook's answer holds the clue to
Apple's brand values. He said:

> For us, it is about doing great products. And when I
> look at what is being sold in the Netbook space today,
> I see cramped keyboards, terrible software, junky
> hardware, very small screens, and just not a consumer
> experience, not something that we would put the Mac
> brand on, quite frankly. And so, it is not a space as it
> exists today that we are interested in, nor do we believe
> that customers in the long term would be interested in.
> It is a segment we would choose not to play in.[7]

Your values determine what you are never willing to give
up in achieving your mission for the business, what is sacro-
sanct for you to the point that you will forgo extra profits rather
than ignore it. Values can include issues such as integrity and
trustworthiness, although you should only choose such values if
there is an issue in your industry around lack of integrity or trustworthiness. In other words, your values should not just be plat-
itudes that every other business might also consider important.

---

[7] www.wired.com/2009/04/apple-coo-revea/

They can also encompass lighter issues such as the importance of having fun when working.

Your values are closely connected to what drives you, and how you manage your business. They impact the culture you create and affect your approach to leadership. To make sure your values provide a key tool for employees, and are more than words in an annual report, it helps to look at how some successful organizations have used their values to hire employees and motivate their performance.

Zappos is a good example to look at. They have 10 values that are incorporated into a manifesto that ensures they can deliver on their purpose. They make sure that everyone who is hired is filtered through their values and the purpose they are trying to achieve. Everyone must be aligned with the values and purpose of the organization. They used their values to create a very successful online store for shoes.

The hard part for most organizations – when thinking about their values and articulating their purpose – is figuring out how to make it more than just words.

Mission or purpose

Business has changed radically since 1962 when Milton Friedman wrote in *Capitalism and Freedom* that there is 'one and only one social responsibility of business – to use its resources and engage in activities designed to increase its profits, so long as it stays within the rules of the game, which is to say, engages in open and free competition without deception or fraud'. In 2009, Simon Sinek wrote the book *Start with Why: How Great Leaders Inspire Everyone to Take Action*, arguing that most successful organizations know why they do what they do. Sinek's Golden Circle envisages starting from 'Why' before moving on to the 'How' and 'What', when thinking through your business strategy.

Your why is all about your purpose, your reason for being, why you exist. It should be bigger than just your product. If there is one thing you are trying to accomplish in the world, what is it? For purpose to really matter, it needs to go beyond an initiative that sits on the margins of the organization. It needs to be front of mind at the top of the organization.

While Sinek distinguishes between mission and purpose, in that your purpose is the meaning behind your existence while your mission explains what you want to do in the world, many people find it challenging to distinguish between the two. In my experience, there is no need to worry if you cannot articulate a separate purpose outside your mission. Instead of getting stuck on this, do what many businesses, including Airbnb, do, and do not worry about distinguishing between your why and your what. Airbnb uses the terms mission and purpose interchangeably and does not distinguish between their what and their why.

The change in the forces that drive business in the new digital environment was already spawning a move away from pure profit-focused business. The economic changes, new technologies, increased globalization and radical socio-political shifts, and now the Coronavirus epidemic mean that corporations are trying to focus their brands on a purpose.[8]

---

[8] 'With shared purpose, EY and Simon Sinek unite to redefine how business operates in the 21st century', www.prnewswire.com/news-releases/with-shared-purpose-ey-and-simon-sinek-unite-to-re-define-how-business-operates-in-the-21st-century-300229952.html; 'Why business must harness the power of purpose', www.ey.com/en_gl/purpose/why-business-must-harness-the-power-of-purpose

Generally, the approach is to articulate mission statements in lofty and high-level ways because the aim behind the statement is to inspire your team and give direction to the business. Big picture thinking is useful to arrive at a statement that expresses in inspiring ways what you want to do in the world. For example, Nike's purpose is not about making or selling sports goods, it is about motivation and encouragement. They articulate their purpose as bringing inspiration to every athlete in the world. They say, if you have a body, you are an athlete. In other words, we are all athletes. Nike's purpose says nothing about their product. Their slogan *Just Do It* instils this inspiration and is much bigger than their products.

The important point here is to understand the difference you make to your customers' lives, and how you can communicate that difference. Your product is just the means to achieve that end state that your audience is trying to achieve. Start with the customer experience and work back to what you can provide to meet the need.

Amazon's mission is to strive to offer its customers the lowest possible prices, the best available selection, and the utmost convenience.

Danone does not say 'We have better yoghurts'. It does not define itself as a yoghurt maker, but as an enhancer of food for humanity with special application to dairies. Brands like Nike, Danone, and Toyota do not focus on their differences but on their higher goals. Danone wants to 'bring health through food to the many' (JN Kapferer, *The New Strategic Brand Management*).

Controversy around purpose and social purpose in business

Purpose is a contentious issue in the world of branding. There is lots of talk around it, and questions about how useful or appropriate it is. Marketing expert Mark Ritson believes that in 99% of cases, talk of purpose is 'total hogwash'. As he put it during our interview for the Brand Tuned podcast in 2021, he believes that it is the result of:

> … Brand managers who are ashamed to sell things, and don't really like going to dinner parties in North London and admitting that they sell coffee or beer, or God forbid, petroleum. So, they invent something that makes them sound better, you know that they are helping to change the world. I am sorry to sound cynical, but it is so pathetically bad. One of the things you learn early from looking at data and brands is that brands are little, little things, no one gives a s*** about them, except the brand managers that run them. And purpose is really a big, big thing… And so it's really sad to see, at the moment, this obsession with purpose. There are exceptions. You know, Patagonia is the clichéd one, Ben and Jerry's, I really like the work of Dole at the moment… their purpose is to get more fruit into the American diet, that's a great purpose. And there is more to it than just making money. And it's something they can deliver on.

Branding expert and author Adam Morgan, in an interview for my book, disagrees, believing that purpose is not as black and white as Ritson describes:

> There are a number of companies… for whom purpose is pretty intrinsic, actually; it really is born from a truth about the founder or how the company started and, at some level, is still fundamental to a lot of what they do. That is not to say that every decision they make is consistent with it, it is not to say that they don't

occasionally get CFOs, who… cut the edges off here or there. But overall, purpose is an important lightning rod for decisions, and a decision-making tool for the CEO, a part of how they shape their culture and what they do. And then there are a whole number of other brands who have purposes that are entirely cosmetic, that have no real internal clout at all, that are paraded as relevant to the consumer. And yet we talk about the purposes of both those together. I think most challengers that I have studied, if not all of them, have had a sense of purpose. They did not always call it purpose, but they had a kind of a burning sense of zeal about something that they wanted to put right in the category or in the culture. And that has been right at the heart of what allowed them to attract the right people, keep those people motivated, push through road bumps that the world or the category or the market leader or the retailers threw in the way, it was absolutely fundamental. And equally, if you talk to people like value investors… it's very striking that they say, well, we want to invest in brands with a mission/ purpose at the heart of it.

Morgan made an interesting point that, increasingly, big companies have come to ape smaller companies. To quote him again:

So you could argue that purpose in a large company is really the industrialization of idealism… you could argue that the informal friendly chat that your… anonymous electricity provider gives you is an attempt to mimic the human friendliness of a small human brand.

On top of this controversy is the idea of social purpose in business. While having a social purpose makes sense if you can identify a social cause that means the purpose of your product or service goes deeper than solely generating sales (such as an integrated cause strategy like shoe business TOMS' 'sell one, donate one' purpose), it is a bad idea to try to run with a social cause if it is not authentic to you because it is unlikely to work if you just use it as a marketing stunt. Only about 10% of businesses can justify a social purpose-driven approach, such as the likes of Patagonia or TOMS. Patagonia is a great example of this – in fact they arguably exist not to make sales but to save the planet. They think beyond 'saving' to repairing the planet, which fits well with their overall philosophy. Patagonia's commercial operation is truly subservient to their purpose.

For the rest, though, thinking about their purpose does not need to be mixed up with a social purpose. What your purpose thinking should be about is more for the benefit of your team rather than needing to be externally driven. It is possible to have an inspiring purpose for your team without needing to have a social purpose.

In fact, I would go so far as to say that the biggest error made around purpose is to muddle brand purpose and social purpose. They can be one and the same thing, but you must be able to recognize when that is – and is not – the case. Greenwashing, purpose-washing, cause-washing, woke-washing – whatever you want to call it; inauthentically pretending to have a social purpose is bad for the branding industry. Fake purpose is dangerous. The hype around purpose is giving it a bad name in some quarters.

Take home messages

- Create a business plan that sets out the problem you solve, which customers you solve it for, and what your stance will be.
- Work out your business strategy: what business model you will use; how you will overcome obstacles; how you will build a sustainable advantage over the competition.
- Decide a clear vision for your business, focused on the business you are creating and your reason for doing so.
- Select your values (ideally three) about the type of products or services in your category, by reference to who you are and what problem you want to solve.
- Set your mission or purpose (not necessarily a social purpose), starting with the customer experience and working back to what you can provide to meet the need.

CHAPTER 6

What business are you really in?

Every major industry that once was a growth industry and then declined saw their growth threatened, slowed, or stopped *not* because the market was saturated but because there was a failure of management. To avoid this, Theodore Levitt in the book *Marketing Myopia* (2008) argues that companies should stop defining themselves by what they produce and instead reorient themselves towards customer needs. Think about the business you are really in and whether you can better meet the needs of your customers.

An example of an industry that did this well is the cinema industry. In my childhood, an outing to the cinema invariably started with a visit to nearby shops to buy sweets, nuts, and drinks to consume in the cinema because cinemas did not sell foods. Today, a visit to the cinema is a completely different experience. Cinemas generally offer an array of food and drinks for customers to purchase before they go into the auditorium, and some cinemas have transformed the experience inside the auditorium too by installing a bar area. Instead of the traditional rows of uncomfortable seats, they provide roomy armchair seats, some of which even have small tables between them on which to put your food and drinks. The experience is more like a bar restaurant. Cinemas have thereby created revenue streams that did not previously exist, and far exceed the amount they receive from ticket sales. Additionally, they are better serving the needs of their customers.

Asking ourselves this question of what business we are really in does not just stop at identifying new opportunities. Technology is changing the world at a rapid pace, and it is possible that thinking about your business from other perspectives will give you fresh insights to draw upon. It could impact your very survival as a business, as is all too clear when you consider a business such as Kodak. Had Kodak focused on this question at senior management level, it might have decided that it was not just in the film business but in the memory preservation business. By defining themselves and their role more widely to reflect what their customers were trying to achieve, they might have reacted more appropriately to the changing technological landscape. Framing their business as being all about the preservation of memory would have called for different products and solutions. Those products would have changed with the times. Instead, Kodak focused on preserving its existing revenues instead of understanding and then meeting customer needs.

Although it is not an easy question to answer, it can make or break your business to understand what business you are really in. It is natural to focus on the products and services that made you successful, and where your resources have gone, or where your knowledge lies, but a better approach is to think about the real difference you want to make to someone's life, rather than focusing on your products and services. It helps to discover what customers are feeling when they interact with your business, and to know what they are after. What is the better version of themselves, the ideal they have for their lives? This will reveal how you can fill that gap and help them get there.

But it is by no means easy to understand what customers want and whether it is time to update your thinking about the relevance of your category.

Case study: Rand Fishkin & Moz

In his book *Lost and Founder: A Painfully Honest Field Guide to the Startup World* (2018), entrepreneur Rand Fishkin explains that his business strategy for Moz at one stage involved developing various related online products – his thinking being that SEO had reached its peak, and that it was both appropriate and prudent to diversify into related offerings. Nobody wants to be the next Kodak, after all. However, what actually happened was that the company's attention was diverted away from SEO, their strongest and main service offering, and this ultimately proved to be misguided. In retrospect, Fishkin now believes that a sounder strategy would have been to become the world's best at SEO, and not lose focus on its core advantage. And he may well be right – SEO was, and remains, extremely important. This just goes to show how difficult it can be to read the market accurately and work out the right strategy.

Understanding the business you are really in involves orienting your business product or service towards the market around customers' wants and needs. This is known as market orientation, a term coined by Peter Drucker in his 1954 book *The Practice of Management*, where he argued that it is crucial to understand the customer's point of view. Drucker believed that a market orientation is key for all areas of a business to have. It is not just relevant to the marketing department. As he put it: 'Concern and responsibility for marketing must permeate all areas of the enterprise.'

Instead of relying on our own assumptions and hunches about customers (which, in my experience, are almost always wrong) we should do research. Market orientation involves finding out, anticipating, and satisfying our customers' needs by making a concerted effort to understand what they want. To do this, it helps to have in mind a product or service and the category it falls into. Although you do not want to define or limit your business by the product or service you currently offer, what you are currently selling will impact the research you need to do so that you can understand your customer and know whether to invest in that product or service or diversify.

Difference between a product and a service

Broadly speaking, a product is a physical, tangible item, such as a box of chocolates or a car. It can be seen, and, depending on what it is, it might also be felt or smelled. It is usually something you can touch and hold. As such, it is easier to assess what it is you are buying and to have a clearer idea of its likely quality when you are buying a product. A service, such as branding or marketing, is intangible. It arises from the output of one or more individuals and is not generally something you can feel or try out before buying. This is the simplest definition.

However, there are products that are *not* tangible – such as software. That is where it becomes helpful to think about what the customer gets for their money. Generally, a product is a *thing* that you get in return for money – and usually, once you have bought it, the thing is then yours. A service is *time and expertise* in return for money, and although the results of the time and expertise are yours, the time and expertise itself is not.

If that was not enough, there is an additional layer of complexity. Just like software is intangible but a product, it is possible to 'productize' a service so that it takes on a more tangible feel than a service normally has. This involves charging for the service in a different way to distance it from the hallmark of services, namely charging on a time-for-money basis. Apart from giving it a fixed price, other key steps to take to productize a service include:

- explaining upfront what the service comprises and having a predefined process for delivering it,
- detailing the scope of the work it covers,
- giving it a distinctive name, and
- describing the outcome and benefits people can expect from buying it.

When a service is productized, it takes on a personality of its own and can acquire a reputation like a tangible product. A service-based product is less dependent on the individuals involved in delivering aspects of the service – remember, a true service is about paying for time and expertise. If the service you are offering is more about the result that the customer gets, if it is more tangible than simply your knowledge and time and looks roughly the same for every customer who buys it – it may well be that your service has been productized.

This might seem overly complex, but the clearer you are about the product or service that you are bringing to market, the better you are able to ensure the offering is aligned to buyers' wants and needs. Knowing what you are offering will help you decide what kind of research to conduct.

Category

I have mentioned the word 'category' a few times in this book, such as category entry points in chapter 4. It is worth looking at this word in more detail here because the category or sector in which your product or service sits sets the context for your research. It determines the market you need to understand.

Foods are in a different category to cosmetics, which are in a different category to professional legal services, and so on. For example, if we look at a cafe, the category is restaurants of the same type. For biscuits, it is the biscuit category and so on. However, beware of defining the category too narrowly – if you think too niche, you could miss some customers or competitors who matter to your day-to-day business.

Knowing your competition is key to understanding the market and buyers of the category. Competition is not just direct competitors, but also indirect competitors who may have offerings that enable customers to achieve similar outcomes to those you provide – even if their offering is entirely different, if the customer outcomes are similar, they are a competitor. When researching the category, focus as much attention on the alternatives that buyers turn to as you do on direct competitors. For example, McDonald's is in competition with all fast-food outlets, not just with other burger bars.

Jenni Romaniuk, in her book *Building Distinctive Brand Assets*, gives the example of a cafe that serves lunch – and suggests finding out why people go out for lunch. What situations and contexts are they in? What are the buying situations for cafes like yours? What are the alternatives that compete with your cafe? You might look at takeaways nearby, as they are an option that could lure people away. To unearth buyers' wants and needs involves understanding when, and in what contexts, people look to buy the type of product or service you offer. You do not want to limit your understanding to the customers of your brand but to get an understanding of the customers in the wider category. By digging deep to understand the category buyer – why they are thinking about buying, what needs prompt them to search for a solution in the category, and what moves them to buy – you can get a better picture of the category's entry points.

An excellent approach to understanding why buyers buy is explained in the book *Competing Against Luck* (2016) by Clayton Christensen. The approach is to consider what job the customer is hiring this product or service to do. Using this approach McDonald's was able to understand that the job people were 'hiring' milkshakes to do in the morning was as a snack to cure the boredom of their long commute. A milkshake took longer to consume than alternatives and therefore better suited commuters' needs.

Buyers have basic needs that every offering in the category must meet. These are the 'table stakes' that your offering must provide. Beyond these core features and benefits, there are then some additional benefits you might provide to suit the wants and needs of some of the category buyers particularly well. That is why it is important to understand the wants and needs of different category buyers.

High consideration and low consideration

In her book *Buyer Personas: How to Gain Insight into your Customer's Expectations, Align your Marketing Strategies, and Win More Business* (2015), author Adele Revella highlights that whether your product is a high- or low-consideration buying decision has a bearing on the type of research you need to do. This is because buyers invest more time and energy (that is, they engage in system 2 thinking) to evaluate their options when buying a high-consideration item, such as a car, evaluating a new technology architecture, or deciding on a school for their son or daughter. Often high-consideration purchases require a substantial financial investment, and the outcome of the decision will profoundly affect the lives of others well into the future. The buyers tend to thoroughly analyse the various options before they arrive at a conclusion. Typically, they will also need to be able to defend or discuss that decision with others whose lives will be impacted by the decision.

Low-consideration decisions, such as which soap to buy, often need much more complex methods of research to understand because someone's thoughts about an impulsive or low-consideration buying decision usually reside in the realm of the unconscious.

Depending on your product or service, you may need to make use of complex algorithms that examine buyers' online behaviour, or choice modelling and ethnographic studies that attempt to examine mindsets that people cannot explain, even to themselves. On the other hand, high-consideration decisions can be much simpler to explore, as the buyers have already done much conscious and deliberate thinking.

We will look next at some different types of market research, but while we explore these things, it is worth bearing Revella's work in mind. For example, she suggests that for high-consideration buying decisions, the most effective way to conduct your research and build buyer personas is to interview buyers who have previously weighed their options, considered or rejected solutions, and made a decision similar to the one you want to influence. Interviewing 10 customers or prospects is sufficient, and the only scripted question you need is the first one, namely: Take me back to the moment when you first became aware that you needed a solution to help you with... When did you first realize there was a problem that needed to be solved? Tell me about the triggering event that led to your search for a solution like mine. (This would have happened well before they ever encountered your business, so you want to take them back in time to before they bought from you and find out whether they considered any other options.)

Revella's methodology provides a powerful way to orient your business activities towards *your* market, so that you can create buyer personas: that is, you can pick the people who most love or need your product and will need the least convincing when you market to them. They are already looking for what you offer. We will come to buyer personas in more detail near the end of this chapter.

Types of market research

To understand your market, you need information to help you make better decisions. Market research for larger businesses will differ to the type of research a smaller business might be able to afford. Some research is always better than none, and it does not have to be expensive or complicated. You might glean valuable insights into a problem or opportunity and how the market sees an issue by simply doing Google research. See what competitors are offering, and the problems they are addressing. Then, once you understand the larger market issues, you might put together specific questions on which to gather information that leads to your new product or service.

Here is some basic information about different types of and approaches to market research. It will help you know what you are buying if you enlist third parties to do research for you so you get the most out of your budget.

Research involves drawing from both qualitative and quantitative data to get a better understanding of consumers, the competition, and the market. You could gather this data from either a primary or a secondary source.

Primary data is data collected yourself, whatever that data is.

Secondary data is collected from another source, such as from reading surveys conducted by another company, or by viewing tables that have been produced by someone else.

Quantitative data is about the quantity – in other words, this is data that is hard numbers and provable facts. How many people, where from, are they female or male or other, etc.

Qualitative data is about the quality. This is about things that are less hard facts and numbers, and more feelings and opinions. How does your target market feel about things? Do they like your product? Do they have any fears or worries?

Often a small business owner will get their quantitative data from a secondary source – for example, they could gather primary qualitative data and secondary quantitative data. The information gleaned from talking to prospects and customers, or observing them, is invaluable in understanding people's feelings, perceptions, and observations about your brand and products. Such information gives you an idea why customers make brand choices.

How you approach research depends a lot on the product or service you have in mind. For example, is the nature of the product or service limited by geographic area, or could you sell it globally? What type of people do you think will buy from you?

Which competitors or alternative providers are there for buyers to consider?

Secondary data sources can be invaluable for gleaning industry trends or shifts, noticing changing consumer needs and preferences, and gaining insights that might shape where your business chooses to focus its efforts and resources. Some secondary sources include:

- Industry associations and trade groups – most associations publish reports or annual outlooks
- Trade journals specific to the industry – bodies like Mintel, Euromonitor, Keynote, and Datamonitor produce industry reports that might give you a view of the market you are competing in
- Government reports – such as the Census
- Market research – such as YouGov
- Industry analysts – these individuals monitor the performance of public companies in your space
- University faculty members – some research reports are published
- Competitor materials aimed at potential customers – these may share useful statistics and reports
- Social listening – this may yield useful insights

Qualitative research methods

Qualitative research methods typically include interviews, observation, surveys, or focus groups.

Interviews are an excellent way to do market research. If you do nothing else, try to conduct some interviews to better understand your buyers' preferences. What are their reasons for deciding to solve this kind of problem, or to achieve this kind of goal?

Observation means you watch how a subject interacts with your product. For example, if you have a software product you might get valuable insights from watching how people interact with it. Or if your aim is to improve eating habits in a school canteen, you might watch students in the canteen at lunch to learn about their eating habits or food choices. Depending on your product or service, observation may be an appropriate type of research or not at all relevant to do.

Surveys involve asking customers a series of questions to better understand how they feel about a product's features, or about the experience they had when using your product or service. Asking good questions is the key to gathering information that is useful, and, ideally, they should be questions that can be shared by phone, in person, on a card or paper, or online using survey software. Surveys are very hard to get right because they are so often unthinkingly and poorly constructed, leading to biased or unreliable information. So, unless you are experienced at creating surveys, it may be worth looking at resources such as Survey Monkey, which have pre-populated survey questions to fit various types of common survey needs.

Focus groups involve bringing together groups of people (usually 8–12) with a common characteristic, to better understand their likes and dislikes. A moderator poses questions for the group to discuss. A use case for focus groups is to get feedback on a new product, new features, or a new ad campaign.

Market segmentation

The need for research might come up at various junctures in your business journey, and much depends on the stage you are at in your business. When you create a product or start a business, your purpose is to solve a problem that is a pressing need for customers. So, once you have identified a problem to solve with your product or service, it makes sense to target the group of potential customers that is most likely to buy from you.

You do this by *segmenting* customers – taking the large 'pie' that is the available market, and metaphorically cutting it into pieces or segments, based on their needs and actions. Once you have divided all potential customers of a product or service into smaller groups, you can decide which one or more of those niche groups to target. Therefore you:

- do some initial market research to help you segment the market; and
- once the market is segmented, do further research (or use existing research) to decide which segment or segments to target with your product or service; and
- having identified your segment, maybe conduct more in-depth research to really get to know them, find out what their wants and needs are, and identify the problem that you want to solve for them. You can then create buyer personas and design a product or service to meet that need and solve that problem.

The objective is to define and focus on the customers who *really want* what you are selling; those who will most rapidly buy your product or service. For example, if you are selling cars, the potential customers in your category might be everyone aged 21–65 who drives cars. That is a *huge* market, and very disparate and diverse. So, you would segment the market to split this large group down into smaller sub-groups. You can then do some further market research to help you decide which segments to target. Not everyone who might potentially buy a car would be an appropriate target if you are selling a high-end luxury car, after all – therefore, a more sensible approach is to narrow down that large group of potential buyers of cars to a sub-set of people who are most likely to buy *your* cars.

A word of caution here – segmentation and targeting are not the same thing and should not be lumped together. They are two separate exercises: segmenting is purely about creating different groupings of the market and categorizing them based on their different wants and needs. Targeting comes afterwards when you choose one or more segments to market to. We will look at this in a moment.

Look for similarities not differences

There are four standard approaches to segmentation that have been used in the past 50 years:

- Geography
- Demographics
- Psychographics
- Behaviour

Each approach has its own strengths and weaknesses, and some researchers combine multiple modes together. Regardless of the approach to segmentation that marketers choose to take, however, the strategy must be *objective led*. Whether looking at a specific demographic, or focusing on a behavioural insight, attitude, or life stage, the key is to be clear about what you want to achieve and resist trading in stereotypes.

When segmentation is done well – with data and skill – it can and does reveal very different customer segments who want different things and see the world and your brand in different ways.

Over-segmentation

Mark Ritson, in a *Marketing Week* article, counsels against arbitrary segmentation, citing the example of Joon Airlines targeting millennials as an example of poor segmentation thinking. 'Millennials' are a popular target segment, but he points out that perceiving a generational group as a segment is unhelpful and builds on differences that do not matter very much at all. Instead, we should look for meaningful behavioural or attitudinal relevance when segmenting.[9]

So how do you do this well? To start with, you should focus on unearthing similarities between buyers, rather than differences. These similarities will have a larger impact on the success of your marketing than disparities ever could. Here is why: market research should allow you to understand what your customers want (not what they do not want). Your research should reveal the different needs in the market, which will allow you to group together the customers with similar needs by identifying groups of people whose values and behaviour are alike in a way that describes them. Once you have grouped potential buyers by their useful similarities, it then makes it much easier to target this group with an answer to their common needs.

Beware, though, not to draw too many false or generic similarities. For example, classic demographics like age and

[9] www.marketingweek.com/mark-ritson-stereotypes-segmentation/

gender – despite being tried and tested for years – are losing their popularity in market research today as the most common forms of segmentation. These factors may have been appropriate in an age where consumer products were sold to mass markets, but nowadays, segmenting a market by age or gender or geography or social class is likely to be the wrong approach for most products or services. They are just too general, and lead to incorrect assumptions – such as, for example, that all 18- to 34-year-old male ABC1s want the same things. This is a very common assumption – but it is just not true! Human beings are diverse and different, and although we have many similarities to each other, these similarities are generally not driven by such wide factors as our age, gender, or location. This flawed assumption and others like it underpin many market segmentation strategies – so be aware to avoid this as it will undoubtedly result in less success for your research.

Here is the good news, though: the wealth of customer data now available means that it is more possible than ever to evolve one's approach to reflect consumers' behaviour, attitudes, and life stage. Many marketers are realizing that a better approach is to segment based on behaviour or goals, rather than on irrelevant characteristics such as age or gender. However, it is useful to also find out customers' demographic details as you do your research so that once you have identified and named the behavioural segments, you can determine whether customers in each segment share demographic characteristics. For example, if you find that most people in a segment are women between the ages of 25 and 35 who work full time you can add this demographic data in your marketing mix decisions – it then becomes a useful additional correlative piece of data, instead of a flawed assumption that drives a flawed strategy.

Targeting and buyer personas

Targeting is about analysing the segments you have identified, to decide which ones make sense for you to prioritize. This decision may be based on factors such as anticipated profits, accessibility, and your company goals, to name just a few.

This is important: *just because you create a segment does not mean you will target it*.

The way to take account of demographics is more subtle than the general advice might lead you to understand. Gender, for example, only needs to be considered relative to your product or service. If it matters whether your consumer is male or female then include it, otherwise there is no need to focus on this detail. The same goes for whether they are single, married, divorced, or have children. When it comes to income, and how much money your customer earns, consider it in the light of other factors such as lifestyle, and materialism aspirations, as well as how much of their income is disposable. It is a question of the

---

[10] www.marketingweek.com/behaviour-demographics-segmentation/

combination of *cost and value*, not only whether the person can afford the product. Would they want to find a way to afford it?

Once you have reached this point, you will have a much less hazy idea about who you are targeting. You can draw on your interviews and give your persona a name and describe them as you would a real person with hopes and dreams. Create your buyer's archetype, a representation of a whole segment of customers, by focusing on the buyers who have the most compelling need for your product or service. What is the number one result you help them get? What are the explicit and implicit benefits they get from buying from you? This is your customer avatar, the buyer persona of the business. It will then attract customers to all the products and services you sell.

When creating buyer personas, think about:

- What makes customers similar to one another?
- What makes them different from everybody else?

Look for similarities and markers that set them apart in these two defining areas:

- They have the same need.
- They base their choices on the same set of criteria.

The number of buyer personas you need will vary depending on the size of your company and the range of products or services you sell. Carefully consider whether you truly need different personas for every small difference that your research revealed; having too many personas becomes confusing and leads to the same problems as over-segmentation. Ideally, you just have one or two personas to work with.

The first customer persona is key to getting insight into other buyer personas in due course. It helps you to find out where your ideal customer hangs out, how they consume media, what social media platforms they use regularly, and a host of other information. This detailed information about a very specific type of customer will help you think about possible messages and the right avenues to reach out to them online and offline. The more you can work this out – including the best language to use, the kind of format, wording, or images they respond to, what their motivation is, what moves them in general in life, and what their priorities, goals, and challenges are when it comes to your product or service – the better your marketing can be.

Take home messages

- To orient your business towards customer needs, make an effort to understand what customers want in the category or sector in which your product or service sits.

- Use quantitative data and qualitative research methods (interviews, observation, surveys, or focus groups) to get a better understanding of consumers, the competition, and the market.

- Do initial market research to segment the market, then do further research (or use existing research) to decide which segment or segments to target with your product or service.

- Group together the customers with similar needs who base their choices on the same set of criteria.

- Create your buyer's archetype by focusing on the buyers who have the most compelling need for your product or service.

CHAPTER 7

The key role of positioning

If understanding the market is about understanding yourself to set your business strategy while also understanding your customers and their needs and wants, then positioning is about what you do to make those two things meet up. The purpose of positioning is to help buyers to quickly understand your offering, so when they are searching for solutions to buy, they can identify why your brand is relevant for the job they are trying to get done. You enable customers to better understand your value by framing what you do, to give it context. People can then know which box your brand fits into. Being aware of the options your target buyers might consider when choosing what to buy for their needs is key to determining which box to put yourself in.

Differentiation and distinctiveness

Differentiate or Die[11] and *Positioning: the Battle for Your Mind*[12] are books that inform people how to position and differentiate their brand. In the 1960s the concept of Unique Selling Proposition was also widely used. Many branding professionals still subscribe to these approaches and stress the importance of identifying a unique brand benefit that competitors cannot

---

[11] Jack Trout and Steve Rivkin, *Differentiate or Die: Survival in Our Era of Killer Competition* (2008).
[12] Al Ries and Jack Trout (2000).

match. They place an accent on being the only one, and on differentiating around a unique benefit.

Byron Sharp's work has provided data from a range of different markets that shows that consumers do not perceive brands as different. It seems that brands are not radically different from competitors in the market. Sharp has thrown doubt on whether differentiation really is such a golden branding objective. The data suggests that distinctiveness should be the real driver of success.

The two concepts mean different things. With differentiation, you are trying to ensure your brand is perceived as different to its competitors. On the other hand, distinctiveness is about having a look and feel that is unique to you, so you are recognizable as yourself, and are not mistaken for other brands in your category. There is an ongoing debate on this topic, sparked by Byron Sharp's book, *How Brands Grow.*

Some branding professionals ignore Sharp's findings and continue to believe that brand positioning is about searching for a single attribute or association that a brand can own in the mind of the target consumer. On this view, brands that succeed stand for things that other brands do not. They own associations that other brands cannot claim. They succeed because they differentiate themselves in the market. Some such professionals espouse brand purpose and believe their brand is there to save communities, inspire peace, create harmony, and so on.

For me, knowing that these are current issues within the branding industry means that when I select professionals to work with on my brand, or to interview on my podcast, I want to find out their position on these issues.

According to Sharp, distinctiveness is achieved by using brand assets that stand out so people can recognize and identify your brand in different contexts. It is about choosing the brand name, logo, colour palette, font, tagline, and images to be distinctive so you stand apart from competitors. Sharp argues that 'distinctive branding lasts, differentiation does not'. He suggests that rather than striving for meaningful, perceived differentiation, marketers should seek meaningless distinctiveness. The research bears him out in multiple product categories. It seems our buyers are no different from our competitors' buyers. So, is it worth trying to distinguish our offering from those of competitors?

To me as a lawyer, it is surprising that Sharp has to highlight the need for distinctiveness. Surely branding is essentially all about distinctiveness? How can you stand out otherwise? However, it seems that so much emphasis has traditionally been placed on brand meaning that often distinctiveness has been overlooked.

The fact that Sharp's research emphasizes the importance of distinctiveness is a double reinforcement of what we already know from IP: that you need to set yourself apart in the name and brand assets you choose to avoid potential trademark conflicts. From the earlier chapters, we already know that businesses should consider competitors' IP, so they can distance themselves from competitors in their own branding choices. Remember why I opted for a ram icon instead of a sextant? Remember the 'meaningless owl' in my Brand Tuned logo? Remember why I highlighted in chapter 4 that it's a bad idea to choose generic names? The emphasis must be on making your branding choices to distance yourself from what competitors have chosen and own. The more distinctive your choice of brand elements, especially your name, the more you stand apart using IP (if, that is, you remember to make IP protection part and parcel of your visual identity creation process).

Having said all that, I would argue that Sharp's findings should not be a reason to ignore differentiation and positioning in your branding when you are launching a new brand. Just because you focus on distinctiveness does not mean you cannot also differentiate yourself from competitors in terms of the stand you take in your business, while being realistic about the extent to which it is possible to differentiate long term. As Mark Ritson puts it, distinctiveness need not come at the cost of differentiation. He outlines the value of working on a tight brand position to articulate how a brand wants to differentiate itself in the market and a set of codes through which they could make their brand distinctive and sees both as integral to brand success. For this dual approach to work there needs to be a huge amount of realism when it comes to what differentiation actually means.[13] While Ritson agrees with Sharp that the accent must be on creating and maintaining salience in the market, even in the most emotional and high involvement categories, he also sees a role for differentiation.

It is especially important when you are a new brand trying to get traction for your idea to think about how you can break through to consumers' consciousness when launching a new product or service. Any initial difference you have that catapults you to success will no longer be evident once you succeed and reach the level of awareness that brands Sharp studied have achieved. By then competitors are likely to have copied your point of difference so that your differentiation compared to your competitors may well become marginal. At that level, what will really matter is that you should be distinctively recognizable as you and that your brand elements stand out. This

---

[13] www.marketingweek.com/mark-ritson-distinctiveness-differentiation/

means your branding should be well chosen and protected, and that you should enforce your rights against any competitor copying them. Until then, positioning yourself towards your chosen market segment, and differentiating yourself from your competitors, will be key to building your brand in the minds of your target market.

Once you have chosen your positioning and differentiation strategy, move on to create a good business and brand. Do not limit your visual branding's distinctiveness by trying to incorporate your differentiation in your choice of symbols. Your choice of symbols and fonts should be guided by the need to distance yourself from your competitors to uniquely stand out, rather than limiting those choices by reference to whether they are meaningful of your differentiation. The differentiation will erode with time due to competitor copying. However, if you have chosen your brand name and assets with distinctiveness as the uppermost consideration, have protected those elements, and have enforced your rights against copyists where necessary, then your branding will remain distinctive. Those elements in and of themselves give you patent-like protection if your product or service is associated with your branding. Here think about well-known brands that stand out in your own mind to understand what job your branding needs to achieve.

What positioning involves

Positioning needs to be aspirational so the brand has room to grow and improve, and, at the same time, it should be based on what the brand is. How you position yourself among competitors, and separate your offering from theirs, involves deciding what you want to stand for and want to deliver as a brand promise. What do you want to give people as the primary reason to choose you? For what group of people do you want to be the obvious choice? What is the use case for using your product or service?

Positioning makes it easier for the customer to make their choice. It helps customers by giving them a shorthand way to find what you uniquely provide or focus on. For example, when there was an array of car brands for people to choose from, Volvo latched onto 'safety' and positioned itself as the 'safe' alternative. They hammered the idea home with dramatic television commercials featuring crash tests. This positioning made them very attractive to a certain group. It would have even repelled others. For example, someone looking for a fast sports car may perceive Volvo as an unsuitable option for them. By knowing that Volvo stands for safety, customers for whom safety is a key attribute have a way to identify the right car to consider. It is immaterial that all cars are likely to be safe. The idea of focusing on one attribute out of all the available options so you attract the right customer to the brand is how positioning worked for Volvo. But as Mark Ritson, a professor of marketing and *Marketing Week* columnist, pointed out, when we spoke on the Brand Tuned podcast, it is an impossible goal to try to own an attribute:

> As for brands owning attributes, unique selling propositions and the like, you cannot own an attribute; I've looked at 1,000 data sets, literally, and I've yet to see any brand own any particular attribute when you control for size. Even Volvo has never owned the safety attribute. It had a relative significant strength in terms of perceptions of safety, but there were other automotive brands, if you control for size, etc., that also had good recognition for safety. All that's possible is to create three associations, or attributes, where your brand could strive to have a significant

perceptual advantage. To achieve that, you must only have a handful of attributes you're focusing on, you have to focus on them for a long time. And they have to be the right ones in terms of your brand and your customer desire and your competitors.

So we need a good understanding of what buyers would do if our offering did not exist. What are the possible alternatives they would consider? What would happen if they simply did nothing about the problem? Can you be a brand to buy from based on an attribute that is important to the customer and that you want to emphasize as part of your brand promise? Are there features and capabilities you can offer that the alternatives lack? Those features should provide benefits for the customer. We need to be experts in the different solutions that exist in the market, including the advantages and disadvantages of choosing them.

Your customers often do not know nearly as much about the potential solutions available to them as you do. By getting real clarity about what customers compare your solution with when they are looking to buy the type of solution you sell, you can know the yardstick by which they define what 'better' looks like.

Mark Ritson emphasizes the importance of creating a tight positioning statement that captures the essence of the offering in a way that is accessible to all members of the organization and appeals to consumers. In his view, if you are successful in this, positioning will drive the company's behaviour to such a degree that 'it will appear in customer research as the things customers notice about our company'.

Positioning is as much about what you choose *not* to do, as what you choose to do. Think carefully about who you are going to serve, and what you are not going to do.

But it is not enough to just focus on the competitors. Knowing the target market characteristics, specifically the characteristics of a group of buyers that lead them to really care a lot about the value you deliver, should be your focus. That is how you can establish whether there are any trends that the prospect is interested in that can help make your offering more relevant right now.

Positioning and differentiation

While positioning helps the consumer to understand what you do and stand for, differentiation – as we have seen at the start of this chapter – focuses on what makes you different to competitors. The accent with positioning is on describing your offerings, explaining how you fit in and what you believe is important. Differentiation puts the accent on identifying your points of difference. Just being different is not enough, though – the differences must matter to consumers.

When considering why customers should choose you, note that price rarely offers a sustainable competitive advantage. Someone will always be cheaper. You might die slowly if being the cheapest is your strategy, so ask yourself: what are other ways you can be different? Adding certain features may not be worth the investment if competitors can soon offer those same features.

Especially if you are in a market where the barrier to entry is low, let us say you are a marketing agency, how will you avoid being the same as all the other marketing agencies out there? What will you do when branding your business to ensure that buyers choose you? What steps might you take to ensure buyers can tell you apart from your competitors? Saying that you are better than others is a difficult story to maintain and is usually subjective and hard to prove. It is better to differentiate by reference to something else. Is there something you do differently that might be attractive to a certain group of customers? Could you differentiate yourself as being trained in IP law, or working with lawyers in a unique way so the client's brand can stand out? Or could you specialize in an aspect of marketing or focus on a particular industry? Are you particularly responsive, so that you can guarantee to return calls within a certain time-frame? Is there something about your world view or the way you do business that you could draw from?

One approach to differentiation is to narrow your focus to one niche (at least initially), or to target just one type of client, to separate yourself from the competition. While it is good to have a big vision for the business and its customers to formulate your overarching ambition, it is essential to focus your resources effectively too. For example, when Amazon started out it focused on books even though its longer-term aspiration was always to be the 'everything store'. Focusing on a niche of books enabled the business to establish itself in book sales and to become known before it moved on to other goods. The business might have failed altogether if it had started by trying to sell everything from the outset – it would not have been differentiated in the market. It is an excellent strategy to think of developing your business niche by niche gradually over time.

Another approach to differentiation is innovation. If you are innovating by introducing something new to the market or category, you will be unique either because you have protectable IP, or because it is an innovative solution. When Dyson introduced bagless vacuum cleaners the company stood out due to its patented technology. With time, competitors have either obtained licences or invented their own versions of bagless vacuum cleaners so that Dyson is no longer the only bagless vacuum cleaner on the market. However, it does not matter that the company's initial differentiation strategy for its product is no longer relevant due to competitor activity. The company has achieved its success and emphasizes its design engineering prowess in its positioning. The company describes itself as a technology company, saying on its website 'Like everyone we get frustrated by products that don't work properly. As design engineers we do something about it. We're all about invention and improvement.'

When you introduce a new solution you might meet a market need or even create a new sub-category, giving you an opportunity to try to be the leading brand in that sub-category. If so, it may be a smart approach to redefine your category as part of your positioning strategy as suggested below. This may be more possible for larger organizations to achieve than for small businesses, though, because of the need to market the sub-category separately to marketing your own brand.

Whatever approach you take: anticipate competitor copying. It is unlikely you can keep a profitable niche or concept to yourself. Competitors will try to capture some of your market share. You should expect your initial advantage to diminish once you have launched your idea successfully. When you look at most markets, you find that the combined effect of all this copying of one another results in brands being similar in their approach. If your name and visual branding is indistinct, and your communications are saying the exact same things as competitors... then you will just sound the same as everyone else, and your marketing messages will be near identical too. Make sure that your approach to branding is distinctive enough so once that happens your name and visual branding sets you apart and keeps you memorable. This is the message to take from Sharp's evidence-based research that says differentiation doesn't last, while distinctiveness does.

Category positioning

To get the edge over competitors might mean challenging the status quo and going where others have not, to try new angles, or describing the market you are part of differently. Perhaps your approach to positioning might involve creating a new sub-category. This is well explained by David Aaker in his book *Owning Game-Changing Subcategories – Uncommon Growth in the Digital Age* (2020). Aaker does not distinguish between a category and a sub-category. For all practical purposes they are the same, and this is the approach I am adopting too. Aaker maintains that, apart from a few exceptions, nowadays the only way to grow your business is to find and own game-changing sub-categories. This approach has been behind the surge in sales or business valuation of many of the companies he discusses in the book. Such uncommon growth involves:

- finding new 'must-haves' that provide a new or markedly superior buying or user experience or meaningful brand relationship;

- becoming the exemplar brand that represents the sub-category and drives its visibility, position, and success;
- building a core customer base that is loyal to the sub-category and the exemplar brand to power growth through commitment and influence; and
- creating barriers to competitors to reduce their ability to become relevant options. Such barriers might include the committed customer base, 'must-have' associations, branded innovations, and a basis of relationships that go beyond functional benefits.

Consider the category you position yourself in, and whether you can create more interest by positioning yourself in a different category or in a category of its own. The book *Play Bigger: How Rebels and Innovators Create New Categories and Dominate Markets*[14] explains that a new category is one that solves a problem people did not know they had or solves an obvious problem no one thought could be solved. Airbnb created a new category. Instead of describing it as being in the hospitality industry, they describe it as in a category of its own, 'community driven hospitality'.

April Dunford, in her 2019 book *Obviously Awesome: How to Nail Product Positioning so Customers Get It, Buy It, Love It*, points out that if you have always thought of your product in one way – as competing in a particular market, or solving a particular problem – it is hard to see it in any other way. The reality is, though, that most products can be many things to many types of buyers. She cites Arm & Hammer baking soda as an example

---

[14] Al Ramadan, Dave Peterson, Christopher Lochhead, and Kevin Maney (2016).

of a product that was repositioned for a different purpose to its original one of baking. As the market for baking began to decline with the rise of packaged foods, the inventors decided to reposition the baking soda based on another of its features, which was its ability to absorb odours inside a fridge. Some consumers were already putting open boxes of Arm & Hammer in the fridge to help control bad smells. So, the company began advertising the product as a deodorizer for fridges. The repositioning drove sales from US $16 million in 1969 to US $318 million in 1987.

Whether yours is an existing business concept or a new idea, positioning your brand in the market among its competitors, and making a clear brand promise, should be part of your strategy for being perceived as unique. For a new brand especially, it is necessary to consider differentiation and positioning carefully. Your point of difference when you first launch your new concept will give you an initial advantage and energy in the market, and you need to take advantage of that initial difference by moving fast to establish a foothold in your market. Your hope should be that you can become the preferred choice by a group of buyers and become known. Longer term it is your brand name and distinctive brand assets that will be remembered by buyers. For the reasons mentioned in Romaniuk's book, *Building Distinctive Brand Assets*, they should be regarded as permanent fixtures, so choose them carefully, avoiding trademark conflicts, and place the accent on IP ownership. That is how you increase the distinctiveness of your branding.

Take home messages

- Give context to your product or service by framing what you do.
- Positioning helps buyers to quickly understand your offering: when they are searching for solutions, they can identify why your brand is relevant for them.
- Use distinctive brand assets to stand out so people can recognize and identify your brand in different contexts (and to avoid potential trademark conflicts).
- Differentiate your business from competitors, using your brand promise to separate your offering from theirs.
- Consider the category you position yourself in, and whether you can create more interest by positioning yourself in a different category or in a category of its own.

Part 3

t u **n** e d

Name it right

Now we are into the third part of the TUNED framework – choosing a name. This is a most important choice you make for your brand – one where distinctiveness is a key consideration.

Chapter 8

Brand naming hierarchy

Before you can pick a name that is right for you, it helps to understand naming hierarchy. The longer-term approach your brand might adopt involves thinking about the relationship between your corporate or master brand and any product or service brands – in other words, it is unlikely that you are naming in a silo, and you will probably have related brands to think about. Even if you are a sole trader, or are starting a new venture, this chapter applies to you because you will have a brand name for you or your company, and you may need to choose other brand names for the various products and services you offer – if not now, then maybe in the future.

A strategic approach

When you have a blank slate and are in the early stages of naming your business or products, understanding the implications of name choices equips you to be strategic so you avoid the need to undo unnecessary complexity that may otherwise arise.

As soon as you have an idea for a new product or service and want to choose a name, think about the long term. Is the name going to be your corporate or product name? Will you use a different name if you introduce a new product or service? Could you just use a single name instead of a new name? When is it appropriate to use a completely different name and brand?

Businesses often choose a company or trading name and introduce new names for their products or methodologies without realizing the implications of their choices. Yet as soon as a business chooses another name it is effectively also making decisions about its brand architecture. Naming hierarchy impacts your budgets and financial resources down the line, so make decisions that will work not just today but also down the line.

Naming hierarchy

Professor David Aaker and his co-author Erich Joachimsthaler introduced a way of understanding more complex brand structures in an article, 'The brand relationship spectrum'.[15] The four main brand architecture types they identified are:

- Branded house
- House of brands
- Sub-brands
- Endorsed brands

The two broad distinctions to be aware of for naming hierarchy is the difference between the 'branded house' (or 'house brand') and the 'house of brands'.

House of brands

The 'house of brands' is where a business with many products gives each one a standalone name. For example, you may or may not know that Procter & Gamble is the corporate entity that has created household-name brands like Tide, Duracell, Pampers,

---

[15] *California Management Review* (2000).

Head & Shoulders, Olay, and more. Each of these brands stands on its own feet. They are branded and marketed individually. This approach has traditionally worked well for consumer companies such as Procter & Gamble and Unilever, although in recent years even they have adopted a slightly different approach, which we will come to later in this chapter. Mars is another example of a house of brands approach. The company founder Franklin Mars named the chocolate product he was creating as Mars. Then as the company introduced new types of confectionery products, they chose new names for them, such as Twix, Snickers, Skittles, Milky Way, M&Ms, Orbit, and so on.

The house of brands approach works well when a company's portfolio targets different audiences with the same product categories, such as three shampoo brands for three different target groups. Using the house of brands approach, it is easier to build different propositions and new associations for each product. For example, one could be a low-cost shampoo, another might be aimed at solving a hair problem like dandruff, and the third could be a premium hair salon shampoo. An organization wanting to create products that occupy both the luxury and low-priced end of the market needs to use different brands to preserve the brand equity in luxury products and avoid damaging the brand with low-priced offerings. So, for example, Marriott's high-end hotels are branded differently to its business class hotel. They use different names: Ritz-Carlton and Courtyard.

This brand architecture requires a substantial marketing budget because building awareness of each individual brand involves promotion of each product under different names. If you do not have the financial resources that it requires to build a separate brand you are likely to dilute your efforts. You would do better to choose the house brand approach described below.

House brand/branded house

The 'house brand', on the other hand, is where the company focuses on one main brand, which runs through all its subsequent product names. For example, Virgin uses the same name across numerous different businesses, by adding descriptors such as Virgin Hotels, Virgin Media, Virgin Records, and so on. The focus is on a single, well-known brand name.It depends on the type of business you have, and the nature of your products and services, as to which approach is most appropriate for you. For most smaller or newer businesses, it is advisable to use the house brand approach due to the additional resources it takes to promote more than one brand name. The 'house brand' is financially more economic because you take one strong brand and plough all your brand meaning into it. You can separate new products or service offerings with descriptors (rather like Virgin does) instead of by choosing separate brand names for them. Let us say Mars went for the house brand approach rather than the house of brands approach that they actually chose. In this alternative universe, we might have Mars Buttons, Mars Coconut, Mars Sweets, and so on. A house brand approach focuses your resources. Any new product immediately benefits from its association with the main brand. It also simplifies the trademark clearance and registration aspect of your business that can be quite a substantial cost once you start extending the brand internationally.

The danger when using the house brand approach is that the brand might be damaged if one of the products develops a bad reputation. If our fictional Mars Buttons were found to cause blue polka dots on faces, then the reputation of Mars Coconut and Mars Sweets would also suffer. As it stands, there is much more reputational separation between a Mars bar and a

Snickers – although they do not benefit from each other's brand reputation, they also do not share the risk.

Which approach is right for me?

For most small businesses, I would suggest that using a house brand approach should be the default option. Despite the shared risk between brands/names/products, this approach overall is easier to manage. Your marketing is dedicated to promoting a single brand, and a single domain name, which simplifies search engine optimization as it is more affordable when you have a single domain to promote. Then as you introduce further products, you can decide whether they need a different brand name and why. Remember though: only use a different brand name if you can devote the additional financial and manpower resources to promoting a separate brand.

While it is possible to change your approach later, if you might want to opt for the house brand approach, then make sure you choose an appropriate type of name to make it feasible to just have that name, plus descriptors. Not all names are suitable for this purpose. Companies sometimes start out with one approach and then adapt as circumstances change. For example, Google started out using different brand names for its different services, and later changed its strategy to avoid genericity as discussed in the next chapter.

Sub-brands and endorsed brands

Sub-brands and endorsed brands are similar concepts, with one key difference: in a sub-brand, the main corporate brand is included in the name. On the other hand, an endorsed brand uses a completely different name and branding but attaches the name of the corporate brand as an endorsement. Sub-brands often use a unique name, but they are associated with a parent brand, which is the key driver. Examples of sub-brands are Samsung Galaxy, McDonald's Big Mac, Microsoft Xbox, Apple iPhone, Amazon Alexa, and DoubleTree by Hilton. While in some cases it is possible for the main brand and sub-brands to jointly drive the brand (such as Sony PlayStation), the sub-brand is never stronger than the master brand.

The reason to use a sub-brand is to give a product an identity. For example, McDonald's could refer to its flagship product as a 'McDonald's double-decker hamburger'. By calling it a Big Mac instead, the product gets a personality of its own, a shorthand description to refer to it, and a way to distinguish itself from competitors that might also offer double-decker hamburgers. The name is the way to separate the McDonald's double-decker hamburger from competitors' burgers and make it distinct. Or a name can be used to forge new paths. Sony used the PlayStation sub-brand to go into the gaming market: sub-brands can have a brand personality that connects with the target market better than the corporate brand does.

The endorsed brand approach is closer to the house of brands architecture. The products or offerings have an entirely separate brand with their own distinct name, logo, brand promise, personality, and brand identity. However, they are supported by the master brand. The endorsed brand is used to promote the product or service offering, but it uses the master brand's endorsement as a quality stamp. The endorsement increases buyer confidence in product brands by borrowing trust from the existing brand reputation and helps the endorsed brand build awareness and trust.

In branding, it is important for a product to have a specific connotation that is related to the brand, to establish a foothold within the market. Google as a name is associated with a search engine. So perhaps Google would have done better to launch its social network platform by a different name rather than using Google+ for the social network. When people hear the name 'Google' they would not associate it with 'social'.

The naming structure of an endorsed brand will put the endorsed name and branding first, followed by the master brand. The logo and branding of the endorsed brand is more prominent than that of the master brand.

I opted for a separate brand for Brand Tuned partly to distance it from legal services, and partly because my intention is to ultimately hive it out of the Azrights business so it becomes a standalone business and brand. As an endorsed brand in the meantime, it benefits from the name recognition that Azrights enjoys.

To illustrate how endorsed brands look, here is how my podcast imagery for Brand Tuned approaches branding. You will note that Brand Tuned has its own branding, and that it uses the Azrights logo as an endorsement.

New trends in brand hierarchy approach

In a 2015 *Marketing Week* article, Mark Ritson highlights a trend towards the branded house strategy. For example, Coca-Cola announced its new 'one brand' strategy, with the various product offerings used only to proffer choice to target consumers. They decided to unite four distinct brands under the umbrella of the Masterbrand Coca-Cola. For many years Coke managed each of its drinks as separate brands – Coca-Cola, Diet Coke, Coca-Cola Zero, and Coca-Cola Life – each had its own communication campaign, brand idea, slogan, and tonality. This move towards a more coherent and consistent brand identity using a single brand with different variants, all of which share the same values and visual iconography, saves resources and likely increases the impact of its marketing.

These articles[16] discuss how Coca-Cola moved to its current approach whereby the variants are communicated as different flavours of the same product and brand.

Similarly, apparently both Procter & Gamble and Unilever have begun to introduce their corporate brands when promoting their consumer brands. The clear separation that used to exist between the parent companies, such as Unilever and Procter & Gamble, and their brands, with the general consumer likely unaware some of the brands were connected to the parent, is therefore changing as these companies move towards a

---

[16] Mark Ritson, 'Coke's "one brand" strategy highlights one of the great marketing themes of our lifetime', www.marketingweek.com/cokes-one-brand-strategy-highlights-one-of-the-great-marketing-themes-of-our-lifetime/; www.marketingsociety.com/the-gym/coke-one-brand-strategy-simpler-and-more-sausage; https://littlebuddhaagency.com/blog/the-brand-architecture-change-that-coca-cola-took-a-decade-to-complete/

more traditional corporate brand focus. They are adopting an endorsed approach to their brands by applying their name to products, allowing their previously unknown corporate brands to create resonance among target households.

If the Coca-Colas of this world realize that it is more effective to focus on building just one strong brand, then it would be a costly mistake for small companies with small marketing budgets to launch new, separate brands whenever they have a new product or service to offer! As we have seen in this chapter, the house of brands hierarchy can only be done effectively with a substantial budget that the likes of Unilever, Procter & Gamble, or Nestlé have.

Similarly, an endorsed brand approach may not be warranted for a small portfolio of brands, because every new endorsed brand needs its own branding and promotion, as well as trademark clearance and registration. Achieving sufficient brand awareness takes a great deal of time and a lot of money. If you have 10 brands in your portfolio, to reach sufficient exposure for each of your brands, you will essentially need a marketing budget 10 times higher than for one brand only. Bear in mind that you will need to factor in the cost of search engine optimization and social media marketing, as well as devoting advertising budgets for each brand.

When is it appropriate to use a new brand name?

If you want to target different audiences, such as when you create a new product sub-category, or a different proposition, the endorsed brand architecture is a good choice. In this way, you can use a new name to help your business break new ground, and still use the power of the master brand to help build awareness of it. As we have seen, the endorsed brand approach does require a substantial marketing budget – but the presence of the master brand does make the job a bit quicker and cheaper than having a completely separate brand in an attempt to build a house of brands.

Remember, too, the reputation risk we looked at earlier, for our fictional blue-dot-causing Mars Buttons? When there is a reputation risk related to different products you own, and you do not want other brands in your portfolio to be affected, the endorsed brand approach is more appropriate. If the fictional Buttons were merely endorsed by Mars, they would be less likely to affect other brands in Mars' portfolio.

Assess your situation before choosing a name

In my experience, businesses are not sufficiently aware of these considerations when making naming choices. They choose far too many names. Being aware of different naming hierarchies, and the strategies, risks, and opportunities associated with them, means that if you still want to go ahead and choose new names for different products, at least you go into it with your eyes open. It may be a better use of your resources, though, to build distinctive brand assets for a single brand, in a similar approach to that taken by Virgin. Consider whether this could be effective for your brand when you are choosing your corporate brand name and remember that it is always possible to make changes if you have already embarked on an approach that you now decide is the wrong one for you.

Take home messages

- The naming hierarchy you choose will impact your budgets down the line.
- There are four main brand architecture types: house brand; house of brands; sub-brands; endorsed brands.
- A house brand approach (one main brand running through all subsequent product names) should be the default option as marketing is simplified and more affordable.
- Sharing the brand name allows all products to benefit from trust in the brand but reputation risk is also shared.
- If you want to target different audiences (e.g. when you create a new product sub-category or a different proposition), the endorsed brand approach is quicker and cheaper than having a completely separate brand.

CHAPTER 9

A naming strategy

People often need a name to get their projects off the ground – which means that names can be chosen in haste. Certainly, in my own case, the name Azrights came about without a great deal of thought. However, we have seen from the last chapter on naming hierarchies that names can have further-reaching consequences than initially anticipated, so it is important not to rush the decision. If your business model lends itself to it, use a temporary name while proving the concept and choose the real name less hurriedly. If a temporary name is not an option, then you will need to either slow down to give yourself time and space to choose an effective name or accept that you may want to rebrand once the business gets started. A rebrand is not the end of the world, nor something to be avoided at all costs in the early days of a business: many famous brands have changed their name early in life. Google was called Backrub until 1997, while Amazon was called Cadabra for a few months before changing to the current name.

There is much confusion around what constitutes a good name, and who is best placed to support a business with that choice. It is widely believed that you can choose whatever name you like, or that you need a creative to help you to choose a name, but you should consider choosing the name your-self under the guidance of an experienced trademark lawyer. I sometimes mentor clients to choose a name that works for their needs. They might use their own lawyers to do the legal searches and registration, while I just provide overall guidance to facilitate their decision. If you do want to take on this job yourself, it helps to understand what constitutes a distinctive name that is ownable and legally available for your business. A common misunderstanding around names is that they need to communicate your differentiation strategy or be otherwise meaningful.

Before we discuss names further, note that it is trademarks, not domain or company registration, that determine the right to use a name. They present challenges and complexities because it is necessary to avoid a conflict with similar brand names. Names are potentially one of the most valuable intellectual property assets you create in your business – provided you choose with IP as the main consideration. So, I suggest giving it serious thought and involving a good trademark lawyer on your team. Trademark lawyers work with names all the time, researching them, registering them, disputing them whether as trademarks or domain names and so on. This experience gives them a unique perspective on names, so they are well placed to help with naming decisions. Involving them early on is a smart move. In practice people relegate them to searching and registering a name that has already been chosen, which is a mistake.

Let us now look at the types of name you might consider using, so you can set your naming strategy.

Purpose of a brand name

The name by which customers identify your company is the first encounter they have with your brand. It is the single most important decision you make for your brand. The name is the primary way buyers will remember your brand. It is the frame on which all your distinctive assets will hang.

According to Forrester Research,[17] 50% of every buying decision is driven by emotion. Not only do we buy things that make us feel good, but we are also inclined to buy things with *names* that make us feel good. Phil Barden highlights the importance of language and its effect on the perceived value of a product, as well as its performance, in his book *Decoded* (2013). He says:

> In a test of messaging on meat packaging, the signal '75 per cent lean' was valued significantly more positively than the message '25 per cent fat'. Interestingly, this higher value persisted when the meat was consumed, meaning that the description influences not only the purchase decision but also the subjective experience of the product.

As he says, we do not explicitly think 'I prefer food served with vivid adjectives', yet a dish's description turns out to be an important factor in how it tastes. It stands to reason, then, that the name you use for your brand will also evoke a reaction.

Factors in a naming strategy

Let us now consider the factors that can make up an effective strategy to help you choose the right name.

Know your category

The starting point in choosing a name is to consider your category. See how competitors brand themselves, and then choose

---

[17] 'A closer look at the monetary value of emotion', https://go.forrester.com/blogs/16-09-20-a_closer_look_at_the_monetary_value_of_emotion/

a name that will stand out from the rest, while still being in keeping with the category.

The purpose of the brand name is to distinguish your goods or services from those of other undertakings. The name is your 'badge of origin', designating the goods or services you sell. As we have seen, it is imperative that the name should be unique; you do not want buyers to get confused about the source or origin of your goods and services due to your choice of name. The name is as much for the benefit of consumers as it is for your benefit. It enables buyers to make buying decisions and choose products and services in the marketplace. If you bear this in mind, you are less likely to believe that you can use a name that is like an existing brand by simply adding a descriptor to the name or otherwise making small adjustments to it. In any event, it is inappropriate to add descriptors to a brand name. Apple should never have added 'Computers' to their name originally so as to need to 'rebrand' by dropping the word Computers a few years later.

Know your market

The right name will be impacted by your business plan and the territorial scope of your activities. Which countries are key for you? What products and services will you sell in the foresee-able future? If you intend to operate in a few different markets and intend to sell a variety of goods and services, you need a name that can be extended easily and is very distinctive – such as Zumba. Had this company used a less unique name for its business, it might have had an expensive journey trademarking it internationally. The effect of a trademark is that anyone who wants to provide something under the trademarked brand, let's say 'Zumba' dance classes, or to use the name for the goods and services for which the name has been registered needs permission (a licence) from the trademark owner to do so.

Had the name not been that distinctive, it is even possible Zumba would have had to trade with a different name in some markets if there were similar names already in existence. For example, Burger King had to trade as Hungry Jack's in Australia for this reason. Even though the Australian company has now managed to secure the Burger King name in Australia, it has wisely decided to stay with the name Hungry Jack's as the name has brand value locally. So, we can see that the type of brand name you choose determines whether the brand is a suitable vehicle for monetization internationally. That is why it is wise to involve trademark lawyers in any international naming plans, rather than assuming that your name is purely a decorative matter.

Know your parameters

When deciding your naming strategy, think about the parameters of your choice, and your objectives – what must exist for you to know you have the right name? What is the name trying to achieve, and how will you know a potential name is worth considering?

What ideas do you want the name to convey? Is there a type of name that you particularly want?

Should the name make people think the product is premium? Are you trying to convey a more abstract concept? What underlying idea or emotion are you trying to convey through the name?

Do you want your company to communicate a sense of fun and innovation, or do you want to create a more traditional impression? Do you want the name to be friendly and approachable?

Will you have online products or a podcast using the name? This impacts the trademark classes and countries in which to secure rights to the name.

When choosing a name, go back to your values and vision, consider your strategic thinking for the business and your target market (if any) – all of this should provide you with inspiration about the parameters for your name.

Types of name

Broadly, there are six types of name to consider.

Descriptive names

Descriptive names inform the world what it is you do.

If the name blatantly describes your goods or services – for example, if you are a plumber, and decide to call yourself The Plumbing Company – such a name is too descriptive to be capable of functioning as a trademark, which means it is a poor choice of brand name in terms of future exploitation and legal protections. Your revenues will be lower when you use a name that is not unique to you. Unfortunately, many founders as well as their marketers are drawn to such names because descriptive names involve a smaller marketing budget to promote the offering in the early days, and because descriptive names seem to work well in terms of forming a mental association in customers' minds with what the company does. However, the long-term disadvantages this entails for a brand are significant.

In the early days of the internet, it was like a small town. There were just a few suppliers in each category: there was just one pet store, one agency, one wine shop, one bookstore, and so on. So, people were drawn to using descriptive domain names because they worked well with early forms of public search engines.

Until about 2014, when people searched for something online, Google would take account of the website's domain address (URL) as an important factor in determining which sites were most relevant to the searcher's query. So, if a site used the same descriptive term in its domain name as the searcher searched for, that site was more likely to rise to the top of the Google search results than a site whose address bore little relation to the descriptive term that was searched. For example, if you searched for 'books' a site using the domain name books. com was more likely to rank at the top than 'Barnes & Noble'. (In fact, books.com now belongs to Barnes & Noble, so that if you go to books.com the domain redirects to barnesandnoble. com). This search engine advantage spurred the use of generic keyword-rich domain names as the internet took hold of our lives. They were very sought after because people wanted to generate traffic to their website.

According to SEO expert and co-founder of Moz, Rand Fishkin, conflating SEO with branding in this way is no longer helpful or relevant for brands.

Think about such examples as law.com, wine.com, and pets.com, which in the early 2000s were raising significant funds. Or think of desktop.com, which had completed its first-round financing of US $29 million; phone.com, with its market capitalization of US $6.8 billion; and buy.com, which was planning on spending US $50 million on advertising in 2000. Despite these huge sums of investment, has anyone heard of these sites today?

So, while using descriptive names may have given you a search engine visibility benefit a few years ago, nowadays due to changes to Google's algorithms, a keyword-rich domain name gives you *no benefits* in search. A generic descriptor as a business name is as unimaginative as calling your dog 'Dog'. Unfortunately, people choose descriptive names, possibly because they do not fully appreciate the serious limitation such names place on the potential of the brand to survive and thrive. Descriptive names ultimately damage your market share.

Case study: US Tax and Financial Planning

When Darlene Hart of US Tax and Financial Planning chose this name, she was the first in the market to set up a business to address the tax and investment needs of US citizens located outside the USA. Not even the big four accountancy practices were offering these services. However, her choice of a descriptive name effectively invited in theft of the business' market share. Competitors soon emerged when they realized this was a lucrative area of business and began to offer a similar service using similar names.

By using a generic name, the business effectively devoted some of its marketing budget to propping up these competitors who arrived on the scene: once people heard about the business, they would search Google using 'US tax and financial planning'. However, as this is a description and not a unique brand name, they would find many providers of the service, using slight variations of the description. They would not always know how to find the original business that had come up with the concept unless they knew that the business was founded by Darlene Hart.

Consider what would have happened if the business had used a distinctive name that did not describe the category. For example, Charles Schwab provides various services to support people with their investment and retirement planning. People who hear of the business and search for it by name would find the company and nobody else. If they searched for the service, investment and retirement planning, they would find various providers. Charles Schwab would also be found from this term as the business does search engine optimization work around these terms. If Darlene Hart had used a distinctive name, such as Hart, then anyone searching for her business by its brand name in those early days would have found her business and not got diverted elsewhere by the search results. The business' reputation and goodwill acquired in those early days when there was not a plethora of existing providers in the market would have gone to benefit her business rather than competitors'.

Despite its poor choice of name, the business is successful. With the passage of time, it has adopted and trademarked the acronym USTAXFS to distinguish itself from the other providers. However, the brand equity the business would have built up over the years would be more substantial if it had begun with a unique name. Its revenues would have been higher simply because of the name. The legal protections that exist against competitors depend on having a unique name.

Using keyword-rich, descriptive names is one of the biggest mistakes people make in branding, because such names do not uniquely stand out. The brand name is *not the place to describe what you do*.

If you want to give buyers some context to understand what your company does then you could use the tagline to do that. But ultimately, your marketing messages and content should communicate your offerings.

Acronym names

Initials are also not the way to go when it comes to naming a business. Often people who used a descriptive name, such as Darlene in the above example, then choose an acronym. It is because they started out using descriptive brand names and when they want to secure their trademark they realize their name is not capable of being trademarked so they then choose an acronym of their former name.

However, problems arise when the initials a brand would want to use are claimed by another brand. This happened when both the World Wide Fund and the World Wrestling Federation wanted to use WWF. The two brands were engaged in decades of domain and trademark disputes in different jurisdictions until the Wrestling Federation rebranded to WWE instead.

Also, not all initials are capable of being adopted as brand names. For example, say you want to use a well-known acronym like ROI or the initials of industry terms, the trademark rules will deem such acronyms as incapable of functioning as a trademark. That means everyone else is free to use the acronym and you would not have a unique identifier for your business.

When you start with a clean slate and have no reason to choose an acronym as a name, then why pick an acronym?

People assume that initials might be a good approach to naming because they want to follow the example of the plethora of household names and other brands out there that use initials, such as IBM, HSBC, BNI, GE, BT, and BA. All of these had descriptive names that were not capable of being registered as trademarks. That is why they used acronyms.

The name is the first contact buyers have with your brand, and acronyms are rarely memorable. They really are meaningless to anyone but the person who came up with them. The well-known ones have spent significant resources in marketing until their acronyms are recognizable. It is not because acronyms are a good approach to naming that they chose an acronym. You would be better off using a made-up name that you like the sound of, instead of opting for an unmemorable acronym.

Suggestive names

Suggestive names appeal to people because they suggest the category without directly describing it. Examples include Geek Squad, Toys'R'Us, Deliveroo, and Hotel Chocolat, plus our very own Brand Tuned. If the name avoids the descriptiveness trap and falls on the right side of the descriptive/suggestive boundary, it can function as a trademark. However, such names are not necessarily suitable for all business plans. They are not the strongest type of name. They are less suitable for international brands operating in a number of categories. Also, they are more expensive for brand protection. EasyJet spends far more than Ryanair on protecting its brand simply because it is more expensive to enforce your rights in suggestive names than in proper names like Ryan.

Real dictionary word names

Names based on real dictionary words that do not describe your product or service are a popular approach to naming. People often assume they can use any common word they like when they are choosing a brand name because they do not believe that an existing brand might have rights over a common word element, such as Boss. Yet choosing an ordinary word as a brand name is all around us. Well-known examples of brands that have based their brand name on a real dictionary word include Apple, Shell, Amazon, Red Bull, Egg, Mango, Jaguar, Uber, Akimbo, and Virgin. These are all words that have an existing meaning. You could draw from a wide pool of names for this approach, including names of Greek Gods, rarely used dictionary words, words that make a nice sound, and so on. You just need to avoid choosing a word that another business has already chosen as the basis of their brand, or at least accept that there is a risk that your use may be challenged down the line. Although branding professionals opt for such names to communicate something about the brand, perhaps the word conveys something about the desired personality of the brand, I would argue that it is not necessary for the name to have such a meaning. Just as with the choice of owl for Brand Tuned it is perfectly possible to create a story around why you chose a name after it is already chosen. For example, I explain Azrights as a name we chose to convey the fact that we provide the A to Z of IP rights and related business law services. However, the name was chosen before the decision about our services.

As Byron Sharp pointed out in a podcast interview,[18] the name McDonald's is of Scottish origin and is hardly meaningful

---

[18] Let's Talk Branding (11 August 2019).

for a burger brand. We use brands to simplify our lives, to be a little box in which we store memories, such as about what the brand provides.

Apparently, Steve Jobs chose Apple when he was 'on one of his fruitarian diets' and had just returned from an apple farm. He thought the name sounded 'fun, spirited and not intimidating'.[19] The word does not necessarily need to be an English word. For example, Zumba apparently means to buzz like a bee and move fast in Spanish. What a name sounds like also conveys meaning. Even if you have no knowledge of what Zumba means in Spanish, the sound of the name suits the activity of dance classes. Pret a Manger (which has now become just Pret) was named after the French phrase meaning 'ready to eat'.

If you use a name that is a dictionary word, the meaning of that word will paint a picture and will itself communicate a meaning to different people, depending on what the word signifies to them and what they associate with it. With time, as a brand becomes established the associations to the original meaning die away. For example, we are unlikely to think of apples when we hear the Apple brand name, or of shells when we come across Shell the brand. Jenni Romaniuk points out in her book *Building Distinctive Brand Assets* that if an asset already has associations for people, the risk you run in choosing that asset for your brand is that consumers will be reminded of those other associations and your assets will not evoke associations unique to your brand. By analogy, the ideal is to use a brand name that *only* evokes your brand and does not evoke other memories that might compete with your brand. This would point to

---

[19] 'From the archives: Steve Jobs in his own words', www.cbsnews.com/news/60-minutes-overtime-steve-jobs-in-his-own-words/

choosing something unique and distinctive – a made-up name, which we will consider next.

Made-up names

A name is essentially an empty vessel into which you inject meaning, so that made-up names are often the preferred option. Names that did not exist before the brand used them are the most distinctive choice of name. Examples include Microsoft, Starbucks, Exxon, and Google, which is a variation of the dictionary word 'googol' (apparently the founders accidentally misspelled the word that they intended to use as their brand name). These brands are using words that have no intrinsic meaning separate from their brand, which makes these words excellent for brand protection. They are often a good choice if you want to sell a wide range of goods and services internationally, and if the existence of a .com domain matters to you. As such names are unique to the brands that use them, if third parties register similar domain names, there are powerful remedies available to the brand owners to recover domains in a domain dispute. Third parties registering such domains are likely to be deemed to have done so in bad faith.

Given that the aim of a name is to create a distinctive brand – what Byron Sharp describes as 'meaningless distinctiveness' rather than meaningful differentiation in his book *How Brands Grow* – a name with no inherent meaning that sounds right for your product or business is a strong choice. The drawback to this approach is that you need to inject meaning into the made-up word. It requires a greater marketing budget than using a word with pre-existing associations. However, it does come with a clean slate, and is a better choice than acronyms.

Proper names

Another popular option is for founders to use their own name. Is it a good or bad idea to name the business after yourself? The research supports both the view that your ultimate business will be worth more and the view that it will be worth less if you use your own name. Although this may feel inconclusive, what it means in practice is that you can be free of worry about the ultimate saleability of your business when it comes to naming your business after yourself, until and unless there is overwhelming research to prove otherwise. Some people say that when you name your business after yourself, your company will seem more personal or familial. If personal service or a family feeling is not an important brand attribute, it might not be the right approach to use your own name according to some branding professionals.

Fashion design labels invariably use the designer's own name, as do cooks. And many well-known household-name brands in diverse industries used the personal name of their founders, including Disney, Dell, Tiffany, Cadbury, Mars, Schweppes, and Dyson, among many others.

Often the name can be made more appropriate as a brand name by only using the surname element. If a business is a success, then it can continue to thrive beyond the life of the founders. Examples of successful fashion labels that have survived include Yves Saint Laurent, Valentino, Dior, Prada, Chanel, Lanvin, and Louis Vuitton. Whether they are continued by the family or are purchased by external buyers, the fact that they endure is a sufficient sign that even a personal brand such as a designer's does not suffer on exit for having been named after the founder.

Ultimately, the key to business continuity is having a thriving business, not whether the business was named after the founder or not. If the business cannot last, it will not carry on the founder's name regardless.

We will consider this approach to naming more in chapter 10, in the context of personal branding.

Taglines and slogans

Although not strictly a type of name, taglines and slogans can provide powerful ways to bring your brand to mind for buyers. Generally, the same principles apply as for names in terms of whether they can function as trademarks. If the tagline does not describe your business, such as Just Do It does not describe Nike's goods, then it will be capable of being uniquely owned by the brand. Nike has had this tagline trademarked since 1994. If your brand name appears in the tagline then there is no problem whatsoever in securing rights to it as a tagline. So, for example, Beanz Meanz Heinz easily qualifies. If there is doubt whether a phrase will be accepted as a trademark, a good approach can be to apply to register it with your name, and then in due course to apply to trademark the phrase on its own. L'Oréal did this by registering L'Oréal Because You're Worth It in 1976, and then they registered Because You're Worth It on its own later in 2001. And if you choose a clever way to describe some-thing, such as John Lewis' tagline, Never Knowingly Undersold, then you can secure a trademark in that phrase. That is how Azrights has managed to register Easy Legal Not Legalese. As mentioned in chapter 4, taglines are useful distinctive assets to develop. Unless you immediately come up with a tagline that fits your needs, it may take time to develop one. In the meantime, you could use a tagline as a way to describe what your business does and keep the name distinctive and unique.

Competitor similarities in name

The first step in the suggested naming strategy above is to consider your competitors. You may well notice that companies in an industry sector tend to adopt a similar naming convention: banks, for example, have traditionally been named after their founders, as have law firms; tech start-ups usually use invented words as names; and restaurant chains tend toward suggestive or evocative names. The name you choose should be in keeping with norms of the category, if any, but at the same time should stand apart from everyone else in the category. Perhaps going *against* the trend in your industry may be a smart move to stand out from the rest of the pack.

An interesting example to look at is price comparison websites. There is Compare the Market, Go Compare, Confused, and Money Supermarket. They all use a similar approach to naming, trying to communicate in descriptive ways what their site offers. While the names are all capable of being trade-marked, the problem with following the pack in the approach to naming is that they tend to be confused with one another. This is particularly problematic, because Google Ads permit compet-itors to advertise using other brands as keywords, so that if someone searches for 'compare the market' using Google, it is entirely possible that adverts for Money Supermarket will be among the search results.

Compare the Market, launched by well-resourced entity BGL in 2006, sought to make itself more distinctive by featuring meerkat characters in TV ads in the UK and Australia. The ads launched in 2009, and according to wiki[20] the site moved from 16th to 4th following the ad campaign. It would be interesting to know to what extent the meerkat characters are unmistakably associated with the correct brand, though. A few people I have asked attribute the campaign to competitors; my husband thought Money Supermarket was the business behind the ads.

Possibly due to the success of Compare the Market, or simply the need to stand out following the use of samey names, other competitor companies such as Go Compare began promotional campaigns too. In Go Compare's case, they used a fictional Italian tenor named Gio Compario (employing a real Welsh tenor called Wynne Evans) to advertise on TV. In their case, the advertisements feature 'Gio' singing the 'Go Compare' tune in various locations and were voted as the most irritating advertisements of both 2009 and 2010.[21]

A new entrant into this market may well think that they have to come up with a character and complex back story in order to compete. However, I would argue that a naming strategy to stand out might be to use a proper brand name rather than a suggestive name, which is the approach all the current category players are using. To be searchable for SEO purposes you do not need a descriptive name. A good SEO company would be able to help you to appear prominently for certain search terms using appropriate content on your site and use of the right keywords.

---

[20] 'Compare the Meerkat', https://en.wikipedia.org/wiki/Compare_the_Meerkat

[21] https://en.wikipedia.org/wiki/Gocompare.com#cite_note-14

Naming dos and don'ts

Do: choose a name that is easy to pronounce and spell

When faced with ordering a menu item people are unsure how to pronounce, many will simply avoid choosing it. If you do not know how to say quinoa and popped sorghum, you would avoid trying to say these words in front of important guests in a restaurant, wouldn't you? Business names have a similar effect. If people do not know how to say the name, they may find it easier to avoid referring to your brand at all. If you have a difficult to pronounce name, you will need to make a point of saying the name on audio wherever possible, so it becomes familiar sounding to people. If it is difficult to spell, consider how you might find a way to communicate how to spell it so you can incorporate that in your promotional content.

Do: ensure the name is brief, and extendible to other goods and services

Does the name limit or restrict you if you were to expand into other areas? SEO Moz changed its name to Moz because it wanted to be known for more than just SEO. As mentioned for Apple, it is the wrong approach to branding to add a descriptor to a name. This is particularly important if you are using the house brand approach and want to be able to add descriptors to the Masterbrand instead of needing to choose sub-brand names. Be careful about rebranding though. Take TransferWise as an example. The company had reached billions in sales and had been operating for more than 10 years when it decided to rebrand to Wise. They believed the 'transfer' part of their name would be perceived as a separate word, limiting their expansion plans. However, it is unlikely consumers who were familiar with their brand were dissecting their name in this way. Just as we do not think of apples when we think of the brand Apple, most users of the TransferWise service would have just got used to the name as a name. Changing the name to Wise, and removing the 'transfer' element, just results in unnecessary cost, especially when it comes to international trademarking, because TransferWise was a more distinctive name than Wise.

Don't: be too ready to change your name

Avoid the disruption of a name change unless you are in the early stages of your business or have suffered reputational damage. Rebranding adversely impacts a business because you effectively suddenly vanish. It is like starting a new business and involves considerable expense. It puts you at a significant disadvantage because consumers will lose the memory associations to your brand and your presence in the marketplace is adversely impacted. If you are unlucky and are forced to rebrand due to a trademark conflict, then it is doubly difficult because you will not be able to simply redirect your domain name to the new one. If your infringement goes undetected for years, it could have more devastating consequences because you will be reliant on the income from the business. Elizabeth McCaughey was required to change the name of her coffee shop in the San Francisco Bay Area, which had operated under the name McCoffee for 17 years.

Don't: use a name that looks like a copy of a household-name brand

McDonald's was able to stop a Singaporean company using the name MacCoffee even though that company had registered an EU trademark. The court invalidated the trademark, saying MacCoffee unfairly benefited from the McDonald's branding by using the Mac element of its name, adding: 'It is highly probable that MacCoffee rides on the coat-tails of McDonald's in order to benefit from its power of attraction, its reputation and its prestige, and exploits, without paying any financial compensation.' As mentioned in chapter 2, famous marks have wider protection than their products and services, so you should avoid using the same name as a household-name brand for your offerings – no matter how much your goods or services differ from the household-name brand's products and services.

The meaning of a name in other languages

If your brand is (or will be) international, then before finalizing a shortlist of names, do some research into the meaning of the name in other languages. American Airlines advertised the luxurious aspect of flying business class to its Mexican customers by focusing on the leather seats, using the campaign slogan 'Vuelo en Cuero' in Spanish. The dictionary neglected to mention that the phrase 'en cuero' is a slang term for 'in the nude'. There was little demand for mile-high naturism among Mexico's business flyers! Details like this were missed when naming the drink 'Irish Mist', which translates in German to manure.

When you are about to finalize the name, give yourself time to look it over, and ask family, close friends, or your team what they think of it. With fresh eyes you might avoid using names like: expertsexchange.com; speedofart.com; or therapistschoice.com.

Domain names

Another decision is whether you must have the .com. It used to be a 'law of branding' that you should own the .com domain of a name you were considering; it was so critical that good names would be dropped if the .com was unavailable. The trademark registers are cluttered with existing registrations, and it can be difficult to identify a good name that is available, especially one that is free to use in other markets too. Nowadays, given that there is a plethora of domain suffixes available, it makes the .com domain less significant. Yet there is still a widespread belief that it is essential to have the .com.

The way people search for companies has changed, and I would recommend not sacrificing a great name just because the .com may not be available. You might be able to buy the .com later; many brands do. In the meantime, they find a work-around. For example, mental health app Headspace used 'Get

Some Headspace' as their domain name until they were able to purchase the .com. We did not own the .com of Azrights until 10 years after starting the business. The way society searches for websites has changed, so that what used to be imperative for the domain URL no longer applies.

Despite all this, if you still have your heart set on owning the .com domain, then instead of unnecessarily purchasing lots of domains until you have made a final choice of name, just find out if the .com domain is available but wait until the name has been cleared for use as a trademark before buying it. I recommend using your browser to check for the .coms you are considering, instead of using domain sites – there is some anecdotal evidence to suggest that domain name searches signal that there is interest in the name triggering some sites to register the name, so that when you go back to buy the domain you find it is gone.

Once the trademark clearance searches establish the availability of a name, buy the domain and be ready to file a trademark application, as well as to register your social media handles. If you do not move fast you could find that while your visual brand identity is being created someone else has applied to register your chosen name or one that is very similar to it, making it necessary for you to choose another name. In other words, the picture might change between your search of the registers and the time when you begin claiming rights to the name – so do not delay.

Organize yourself

When selecting a new brand name, the order in which you do research, buy domains, register rights, and create visual designs can make the difference between having a well-considered brand identity that meets your needs and wasting a lot of time, money, and resources, while still not ending up with a name that is legally available to use.

In practice, it is necessary to have a few names to put forward for legal checks. I suggest selecting three to six names, ideally ones that you have already checked out yourself on Google and via simple trademark register searches. Then send your list, in order of preference, to your lawyers to identify the best name in terms of availability. The checking yourself part is important. When working with designers, we sometimes receive names that are either not ownable or are immediately knocked out when we search the trademark registers. So, if you're working with a designer to name your brand, make sure they only send your lawyers names they have themselves first checked out in a basic way on the trademark registers so your lawyers really do have a range of options to consider.

Understand what to look for when running your own Google checks on names to identify obvious problems. As you do your due diligence to eliminate and whittle down the names, keep notes against each name so you can keep track of the problems encountered with a particular name, and include a list of problems or queries that come up in relation to names that are still under consideration at the end of the process. Keeping a record of your research will help avoid going over the same name later because you forgot you had already researched it. Use a spreadsheet to keep track of your work.

Genericity

People think it is flattering for Google that people use its brand name as a verb, saying they will 'google' something. However, that threatens to make a brand generic so that it could lose its trademark rights. For this reason, Google changed its naming strategy. For example, it rebranded long-standing products like Picasa and Blogger to 'Google Photos' and 'Google Blogs'. New products are now always launched under the Google brand name plus a descriptor: Google News, Google Translate, Google Chrome, and so on. This reinforces that its name is a brand rather than a verb because you would have to use the Google name in order to refer to the brand's products.

Brand names like Aspirin have lost their trademark status in the USA, UK, and France due to genericity so that the name Aspirin is now synonymous with a type of pain killer in certain countries. Other brands that have either completely or partially lost their trademark rights due to genericity include Catseye, Escalator, Thermos, Walkman, Hovercraft, Xerox, and Kleenex. These victims of 'genericide' no longer have a name that identifies the source of their products and services. Their trademarks have lost their distinctiveness, meaning competitors are freely able to attach these powerful names to their own offerings.

Given that the brand is often a company's most valuable asset, if it gets to the stage where it no longer has exclusive rights over its name, its brand effectively dies.

Trademarks

The reason to involve a lawyer to check whether a name is available is to get a legal opinion on the suitability of your chosen name. There may be reasons in law why the name may not be suitable, quite apart from whether anyone else has secured rights over it. Names that are too descriptive cannot function as a trademark, some geographical and common names cannot do so, and some initials may not be capable of being registered either, such as ROI mentioned earlier.

In the same way as, when you buy land, you would first ask a lawyer to do some legal searches and transfer the title to you before you begin building on the land, so you should first secure the rights to a name before having the visual identity created for you. It is a good idea, therefore, to choose the name and secure your rights over it before you reach the stage of having your visual identity designed.

The widespread belief that registration of the brand name as a trademark is something you can leave until your business has taken off and is successful is wrong. Unless you have a significant budget to enforce unregistered rights in a name, failing to register your rights means you effectively do not own your brand name. I have seen how much inconvenience, hassle, and expense people go through when they have not taken this elementary step of protecting the name they are using. It costs 10 times as much, if not much more, to deal with the complications that can arise when you do not protect your name than the cost of registering the name in the first place.

Names and trademark registration are very similar to the ownership of physical property and should be thought of in the same way. If you simply squat on land on which you are developing properties and do not secure ownership of the legal title, your tenure is insecure. You could have the rights taken away from you, or otherwise lose them after a lengthy and expensive court case. Events outside your control might shatter your peace and enjoyment of your property. In the same way you could be stopped from using your brand name if you have not properly checked it out and secured your rights to use it. It is a mistake to regard it as optional to secure your rights to a name you are using in business. Even if you have no ultimate aspiration to sell your business, you should trademark the name you are using.

Society has not updated its thinking about trademarks, so there is a widespread belief that you can postpone securing rights to a name you are using until you have had some success. What is less well appreciated is that by ignoring trademark registration you may save yourself the cost of registering a trademark but, in doing so, you set yourself up for costly litigation if someone else also starts using the name or registers a similar name first, making it difficult for you to co-exist.

The advantages of registering a trademark

Registration of a trademark *considerably* reduces the risk that others will pick the same name. Your registration is on the public trademark registers, and people are expected to search these registers before choosing names in their jurisdiction. If your name is not on the register, someone else may build rights in the same name, and this can lead to messy disputes and unnecessary costs down the line. If you are on the registers and someone else uses your name, they are automatically in the wrong for using the same name. It is therefore a lot cheaper for you to enforce your rights than if you had not registered a trademark. Also, if a well-resourced business wants to use the same name, they will buy you out, whereas if you have not secured your rights, they know that you are on weak ground. In other words, the strength of your rights has an impact on whether you will need to engage in a costly dispute or whether you receive an offer to buy your rights.

This happened to me: as I tend to register a trademark as soon as I want to use a name, I was in a strong position when a well-resourced organization adopted a name I had registered as a UK trademark for one of my products. I happened to notice that they had registered the name in the EU a year after I had registered the mark in the UK. At the time, the UK was part of the EU, so my UK trademark registration took precedence over their EU registration. (In the UK and EU system, owners are expected to police their own trademarks. The system does not stop someone registering exactly the same name.) I wrote to the company in question to let them know that I had spotted their registration and would be applying to have it revoked. The upshot for them would be that they would have to register the name in each of the other 27 EU countries individually and would have to use a different brand name in the UK. My UK registration would block them from keeping their EU trademark. I offered to sell them my UK trademark provided they went ahead and bought it before I had spent time and energy applying to cancel their registration. I named my price, which included the costs of rebranding my project. They immediately accepted, and we did a deal.

The point is that IP rights *matter*. It is not just about who has the most money to fight a battle; it is about who has a strong case. When you have a registration, others are on notice of your rights. While in common law countries like the USA using a mark without registering it does give the user certain rights, it is a false sense of security to rely on unregistered rights. They are a lot more limited and are more costly to enforce than most people realize.

Understanding trademarks

So, once you identify a name that is available for you to use, apply to register it as a word mark (name) in the UK, EU, or in your home country. In the USA and some other parts of the world, the trademark registry only allows your application through if it does not conflict with an existing registration. That means if it is like an existing registered trademark the examiner is likely to raise objections. Therefore, once you secure a trademark in such jurisdictions, it is a big deal – something to celebrate.

Unfortunately, the same cannot be said of trademark registration in the UK or EU, as it is currently possible to register any mark, even if someone else has registered the same name already (trademark owners are expected to police their own brands although they are not obliged to stop others registering conflicting trademarks). Here is an example: Skydrive was registered as an EU trademark by Microsoft. This was infringing on the rights of SKY, who then sued them in the High Court with the result that Skydrive had to rebrand to OneDrive.

Therefore, it makes sense to pay a lawyer to do a legal search and provide an opinion before proceeding to use and register a name. This gives you much more protection than if you just go ahead and register a trademark. That is because in the UK and EU system, existing brand owners who have trademarked a name that you also trademark can ignore your application. They are not obliged to stop you. After you register, if you become successful, they can decide to challenge your trademark registration by applying to invalidate it. They will do this if you become successful, as you would then pose a threat to their territorial scope of protection.

Businesses are often unaware of the lengths some brands will go to secure the broadest possible monopolies for themselves. They enthusiastically file for marks that they believe will not conflict with that of any other brand only to be totally taken by surprise when they are opposed. Whether a legal opinion leaves you thinking the lawyer is being too risk averse or guides you to adjust your branding to avoid highlighted risks, it is better to have insight in advance rather than after you finalize your branding, as it's disruptive to make a change later.

A trademark is the way to get exclusive rights to use your name and will become the most valuable business asset you own. As far back as 1900, John Stuart, the then chairman of the Quaker Oats Company, is reported to have said: 'If this business were split up, I would give you the land and bricks and mortar, and I would take the brands and trademarks, and I would fare better than you.'[22]

Trademarking is necessary for every business

If you do not use a name that can be uniquely owned by you, it means you lack a container to hold the brand value and will have a lower market share. Having a unique brand name is not optional. Even if you are purely setting up a lifestyle business to support you until you are ready to retire, you should think about trademarking your business name so nobody can disrupt your business.

If you have bigger plans for your business, bear in mind that the brand value, as your business succeeds, is captured in a name. You must exclusively own the name and extend your trademark to other countries to protect your revenues in those jurisdictions as they arise. The name protects your market share.

---

[22] John Stuart, 'The value of brands', www.brandwellpartners.com/brandsights/2018/4/9/the-value-of-brands; John Stuart, 'Branding strategy: building strong brands', www.oreilly.com/library/view/principles-of-marketing/9780134492513/xhtml/fileP70010130830000000000000000026C1.xhtml

A strategy for a distinctive name

As we have seen from this chapter, finding a distinctive name for your brand should be the overriding objective. The name will be the primary way people will identify your brand.

Once you identify a suitable name that is legally available, a trademark registration should be the next step so you secure ownership over the name. A registration ring-fences an area of business, giving you exclusive rights to use your brand name.

Registering a trademark for the word should be the standard approach because the name is key in branding. The mental associations that are created with your brand attach to the brand name. The name is the anchor to the brand. Not owning the rights to your brand name is a fundamental mistake to avoid.

Take home messages

- It is trademarks, not domain or company registration, that determine the right to use a name.
- Choose a name that will stand out from the rest, while still being in keeping with the category and your values and vision. Make sure it is brief and easy to pronounce and spell.
- There are six types of names to consider:
  - Descriptive names: too descriptive to be capable of functioning as a trademark.
  - Acronyms: rarely memorable, plus may not be capable of being adopted as brand names and problems arise when already claimed by another brand.

- Suggestive names: can function as trademarks if they avoid the descriptiveness trap but less suitable for international brands operating in a number of categories.
- Real dictionary words: can be used but avoid choosing a word that another business has already chosen as the basis of their brand.
- Made-up names: most distinctive and excellent for brand protection but meaning needs to be injected so it requires a greater marketing budget.
- Personal names are often the most common approach to naming adopted by many well-known marks.

- Select three to six names (checked on Google and via simple trademark register searches) and send to your lawyers to identify the best name in terms of availability.
- Register the name as a word mark (name) in the UK, EU, or in your home country to secure your rights to it before having the visual identity created for you.

CHAPTER 10

Personal, business, and product branding

We usually associate brands with companies and products – particularly with household names like Apple or Microsoft. However, nowadays, even individuals have a personal brand, meaning that for any given business, there are at least three brands in a business: the corporate brand, the product or service brand, and the personal brand of the leader(s) of the business. They are all important for constructing a solid and successful overall brand, regardless of the size of the business.

Personal branding is therefore a necessary consideration when thinking about how to name your business – especially if it is an option for you to name your business after yourself.

What is personal branding and why does it matter?

'Personal branding' is about establishing and promoting what you stand for as a person. If you are a founder your values and ethos likely underpin the approach you take to business. Your personal brand is the unique combination of skills and experiences that make you who you are, and the reputation that you have built. Effective communication of your personal brand differentiates you from other professionals in your field. The notion that personal branding is for celebrities and major companies, actors, musicians, and athletes, and the big business characters like Steve Jobs is quite wrong. The world has changed. Nowadays we should all consider our personal brands.

The concept of personal branding makes some people uncomfortable because it evokes an impression of falseness or inauthenticity. If people spend time thinking about how they want to come across, surely that means they are being artificial rather than authentic? They might be too focused on creating the 'right' impression rather than just being themselves? However, we live in a world that wants to know who is behind a brand. People buy from people, so if you do not take control of your personal brand you are effectively opting to be a faceless organization.

Many founders are introverts at heart and want to focus on building their business. Their natural tendency is to want to hide behind their business brand. They wonder why they should focus attention on themselves when it is their business that should be getting all the attention. The fact is that the CEO of a company is the linchpin and direct representative of the business. Their personal brand supports the business while being completely authentic to the individual in question. It is about building a brand that people believe in, that they care about.

Should you use your own name?

As we saw in chapter 9, many household-name brands used the founder's own name for the business. Proper names are a good option from a branding point of view, as we know, because they are distinctive rather than descriptive, and hence are more cost effective to enforce – Ryanair needs to spend far less on brand protection than easyJet does, due to using a proper name. The question for you is whether it makes sense to use your own name for your brand.

To decide, think about your long-term vision for your business. Do you want to sell the business eventually or do you want a lifestyle business that ends with you?

Smaller businesses should certainly consider using the founder's own name as this provides a significant advantage in terms of making it easier to allocate the necessary resources to promote their personal, business, and product brand. Using the founder's own name means there are fewer names to promote, so your marketing budget can have more impact. If your corporate, product, and personal brand name all use the same core name (albeit adding descriptors to put distance between them), then it will be easier to build mental availability for your brand and to promote the business online using a single domain name.

We have touched on this idea already, but it is probably not worth worrying about whether or not you will limit the future growth of your business by using your own name. There are views that support both perspectives: either that it does not limit your growth and longevity or that, if you want to sell the business, take on a partner, or cede day-to-day management of the company, you would be limiting the new guard's ability to signal their involvement if you named the business after yourself. As there is no clear evidence either way, I would suggest that this is not a factor to prioritize as a consideration when choosing your brand name. As with most brand naming decisions, it matters less which name you choose than what actions you take to make the name signify a brand that is relevant and compelling to buyers.

Other considerations are whether customers want to do business with a company of a more corporate character. Might they feel they are doing business directly with the founder, that is, with a small entity, if the business is branded under the founder's own name?

Given that today founders need to develop their personal brands, common questions that arise are how to tie in your personal brand with the business and whether there is a strong reason to opt for one approach rather than another.

Another key fact to take into account is the suitability of the name itself. The same considerations apply as for choosing names generally. The name should not be difficult to spell or pronounce and should not have anything intrinsically objectionable about it. Nor should the name be a common one; in some jurisdictions, such as the USA, it may be difficult to register a common surname like Smith as a trademark unless the name acquires a secondary meaning.

If you do have a suitable name it is ultimately a matter of preference whether to choose your own name or some other name for the brand – what follows are a couple of examples of when this approach works and when it does not.

Martha Stewart

Martha Stewart provides an example of one downside in choosing to name a business after the founder. A cook who later expanded into publishing and then lifestyle, by 1999 she saw her company through its initial public offering on the New York Stock Exchange. Her stake in the company was reportedly worth US $1.2 billion at one stage, according to *Biography* magazine.[23] Then, in 2004, she was convicted of insider trading-related charges, and spent five months in prison. The company she had established, Martha Stewart Living Omnimedia, continued to try and ride out the reputation hit, and grow in new direc-

---

[23] 'Martha Stewart', *Biography*, www.biography.com/business-figure/martha-stewart

tions, by adding several non-Martha Stewart publications, but in 2015, Sequential Brands Group announced it would acquire Martha Stewart Living Omnimedia in a deal valued at US $353 million. Martha's company had posted losses in 11 out of the previous 12 years.

Martha Stewart's example demonstrates the importance of ensuring that the conduct and behaviour of the owner of the business continues to be impeccable even after they sell the business, because their personal brand is bound up with the brand of the business. The impact would be felt far less from such an incident if the owner of the business were not the name of the business brand.

Gary Vee

Gary Vaynerchuk is an example of how using his own name has helped him grow his social media agency to 1,000 plus employees in just a few years. Legacy is a big motivator for him, so it makes sense to use a variation of his own name for his business' brand, which is called Vayner Media.

The personal brand he is building is undoubtedly helping his agency. For example, it attracts the right recruits and gives him credibility with his big brand-name customers. Using the founder's own name can lead to superior performance for a business, so if you have an unusual name, like Vaynerchuk, you will see an even greater effect in using it to name the business.

Think it through carefully: will your personal brand be the main brand, or will it sit alongside the corporate brand? If you do decide to use a different brand name for your business, how will you manage the resources and allocate your limited budget to build your personal brand and the business' brand?

Resources for building personal and business brands

If you are using a different brand name to your own name, which name should you prioritize promoting? Whether you are building a business to exit, or a lifestyle business that you will work in till you die or are ready to retire, if you only have resources to focus on building one brand, then I would argue that it makes more sense to focus your energies on building your personal brand.

That is because *people buy from people*. They prefer to follow people rather than logos. As I pointed out in my 2012 book *Legally Branded*, people's personal profiles generally have more followers than their business profiles. If you want to build your business brand recognition with a view to one day selling the business, then it may seem at odds with this aim to focus on building your personal brand. However, that is what you would do well to do.

Until you have the resources to maintain two separate profiles independently of one another, a good compromise is to set up an account for your business and use it for yourself personally, by making it clear that you are representing your business. Then you can focus your energies on building your personal brand while still supporting your business. For example, you would use your own photo on your social media accounts rather than your logo. And you would describe yourself in relation to your business – in my case, as Shireen Smith of Azrights or Shireen Smith of Brand Tuned, depending on the business I was trying to promote. In this way, you are effectively an individual repre- senting your business brand. The account name would be your business' brand name not your personal name.

I used this approach on Twitter for a few years for Azrights, and once I had built up a following of nearly 5,000 followers I advised my followers that henceforth I would tweet in my personal capacity over at Shireen Smith and that the current account they were following would be purely used for the Azrights business account. I then replaced my own photo with the Azrights logo on the Azrights profile. Some of the followers followed me on my personal account. Now that I have built up separate identities for my business and myself, I put the accent on promoting business-related content, rather than on promoting my personal profile, but it means I can discuss non-business-related topics on my personal profile if I want to. This is a strategy that could be adopted for any platform – to focus your energies in this way and then split out the identities later when you have more resources. Until recently I have done most of my blogging on the main Azrights site for search engine optimization purposes, although now that I am developing the Brand Tuned brand, this is changing as I put the accent on building the brandtuned.com presence. However, I make it clear on my personal blog that I mainly blog elsewhere although I might occasionally write a blog on my personal site if the subject matter is less relevant to the Azrights or Brand Tuned blogs.

Generally, whether you have a combined business and personal identity, or just a personal identity, avoid posting personal updates (such as about what you ate for breakfast) on your business profile. Keep it strictly business related, because people will be following you predominantly for your business content if you are branding yourself as your business. If you must post purely personal updates about what you ate for breakfast and the like, then do it purely on your personal platform.

The personal brands of founders

If the personal brand is to be the main brand, such as Tony Robbins, then the master brand will be Tony Robbins, which would then endorse any separate product brand names (remember the endorsed brands model from chapter 8?). If, on the other hand, you want to choose a corporate brand name, then you would need to promote your personal brand separately. Your situation would be more like Elon Musk's brand, which uses a separate business name, Tesla.

Elon Musk has created such a powerful personal brand that overshadows his own companies. He has done an amazing job of crafting his own separate brand. Inevitably, your personal brand will impact your business even though the business has its own separate name. Musk is showing you his personal story through his company brand. The vision of his company is a direct result of his personal goals. The strong connection between Musk and his audience is a crucial part of the brand he has built and the story that he is telling. When that purchase gets made, the customer instantly becomes a part of Musk's story. They are taking on these amazing qualities, such as being future-focused and environmentally conscious. They are joining Musk on his quest to move humanity forward. And in doing so, they become the heroes of their own stories. Musk is just the guide on the journey. The customer gets to show people their own values and story through the action that Musk inspires them to take.

This is the key bit: a personal brand is *not about making sales*. It is about standing for something, connecting with people, and getting them to engage with your vision. Your story becomes a part of their story, and vice versa. And when that happens, your personal brand becomes even more powerful. While you want to build a business, you also want your audience to connect to you. You want people to care about your story.

Oprah Winfrey has become a household name that inspires and helps millions of viewers to live their lives to the fullest. She wanted to be a teacher and to be known for inspiring her students to be more than they thought they could be. Her personal brand is about being true to oneself. She has managed to engage with her audience using real, inspiring stories from the lives of people her audience can connect with. Her brand values are about how she can motivate others to find their calling. The real work of our lives is to become aware and awakened – to answer the call – and that is how she works to make her audience's lives better.

Branson is described on his own Facebook page as 'a tie-loathing adventurer, philanthropist & troublemaker, who believes in turning ideas into reality'.

Bill Gates' philanthropy is a trait that colours his personal brand in a very distinct way. Gates' commitment to philanthropy is undeniably his brand's defining trait and one that is reflected in his content, visuals, and social media strategy.

Greta Thunberg is a climate activist, who started the *school strike for climate* movement at the age of 15. The Swedish teenager has made big, personal lifestyle changes to save the planet, such as going vegan, persuading her parents not to eat meat, and opting out of air travel.

Michelle Obama is an accomplished lawyer who was an influencer long before her husband held America's highest office. In the years following Obama's presidency she has built her personal brand by writing books and maintaining a high profile on social media. Her purpose is to advance women. She has a great passion for this cause and believes that the cause has come under direct attack in recent years. It is this passion that encourages so many to connect with her on an emotional level. She is showing people how attacks on women hurt even those in positions of high standing. In that sense, she relates her message to everyday people and inspires and influences them.

Amal Alamuddin Clooney is a well-known human rights lawyer who was born in Lebanon. She and her family moved to the UK, where she grew up and was educated. She has been involved in many high-profile cases, such as Julian Assange, and has a strong commitment to conflict management. She became famous outside the legal community when she married George Clooney. It is clear from interviews of George Clooney that he holds her in high esteem for the work she does. She believes that the background you come from is not the obstacle to success. It depends on the way you use it. She is an example of how a woman does not need to lose her femininity to be equal with men. She believes that everything is possible if one works hard. She is noteworthy also for not maintaining any personal social media accounts, which reflects her low-key approach to personal branding.

From these examples, it is clear that there is scope to develop your personal brand in line with your preferences and style. The important point is to understand what drives you and what your purpose is for doing what you do, and to use that insight to build your own and your business' brand authentically in ways that feel right for you.

When you have a personal brand, people connect to you on an emotional level. That means your emotions can influence theirs, and that benefits your business' brand.

Take home messages

- Your personal brand is the unique combination of skills and experiences that make you who you are, and the reputation that you have built.
- People buy from people – take control of your personal brand to avoid being a faceless organization.
- Using the founder's own name makes it easier for small businesses to allocate resources for promoting their personal, business, and product brand.
- The name should not be common or difficult to spell or pronounce or have anything intrinsically objectionable about it.
- A personal brand is not about making sales. It is about standing for something, connecting with people, and getting them to engage with your vision.

Part 4

t u n e d

Establish the brand strategy

In this part, we will look at establishing a brand strategy that serves and builds on, but is distinct from and separate to, your business strategy.

CHAPTER 11

How to design your brand strategy

A brand can easily be a business' most valuable asset. Here is an example: when the UK-based Arcadia group went into administration and was put up for sale, the business owned leading high street businesses like Topshop, Topman, and Miss Selfridge. Asos, an online retailer, agreed a deal to buy some of the assets of the business. They paid £295 million, of which £265 million was for the brands alone. Only £30 million of the total price was to buy the physical stock. They did not even buy any of the physical stores, as Asos only operates online. Think about that: £265 million of value purely for the brand, an intangible asset consisting of a name and visual identity that contains all the associations people have with the brand, which encourages them to buy goods sold under that name. Given how important a brand can be, then, it makes sense to establish a deliberate strategy for your brand rather than leaving it up to luck.

Business strategy vs. brand strategy

Many businesses do not distinguish between their business and their brand strategy. In fact, it is important to note that business strategy is often not what a brand strategist can help with. At the big company level it's the McKinseys of this world that a business would turn to for support with strategic business help, while at the small company level you need marketers or business coaches with a substantial background in business to support you to better develop your ideas so you can create a successful business. Much of the work you would do on your business will be useful when it comes to establishing your brand strategy as there is an overlap in the considerations for both types of strategy. Therefore, much of the advice in part 2 will also be relevant to brand strategy. When you consider brand strategy, bear in mind the matters discussed there in terms of your vision, mission, and values. Business and brand are two sides of the same coin.

However, as we have seen, if you do not first focus on developing a business model that works and go straight to thinking about the brand, the danger is that you get visual designs in the belief that this is enough to create a brand. That risks ending up with a shallow brand. The thinking needed to determine your brand strategy goes much further than there is scope to cover during a visual identity exercise. That is why the TUNED framework puts the accent on the business strategy first and focuses on brand strategy separately once you have done much of your thinking work.

Designing the brand

A newly created business has no background or history. It will develop a brand that you influence partly through your own personal brand as founder of the business.

A brand gets its coherence from the founder's vision and values. So the starting point is to focus on the founder(s) philosophy and purpose for wanting to solve the problem their business is aiming to solve. Uncovering the motivations of the founder(s) helps in deciding the business' brand strategy.

Whether you are a new business, or an existing business, what is important when working on your brand is to be clear why the business was started in the first place. What you want to stand for and are willing to promise (albeit implicitly) involves understanding the founder or founders' initial motivations if they are still involved. What did the founders believe, what was their purpose in starting the business? For established businesses where the founders may no longer be in the business it pays to go back to the heritage of the business to uncover its roots.

A brand is made over time. Brands become credible only through the persistence and repetition of their value proposition. BMW has had the same promise since 1959: the ultimate driving machine.

Build on your business strategy

Establishing your brand strategy involves articulating what the brand stands for and the promise it holds out to customers and identifying your top values and the brand's personality. These need to be congruent with your actions in business. The brand strategy directly serves the business strategy – they need to marry up. If, when establishing your business strategy, you prioritize identifying the optimum business model and competitive strategy for your business idea, then when it comes to deciding your brand strategy you will have already done much of the groundwork to decide your brand strategy.

To help you do the requisite introspective work, here are some questions to prompt your thinking:

1. Why does this brand need to exist? What would the market lack if it did not exist?
2. What is our long-term vision of the product category?
3. What do we want to change in people's lives?
4. What are our highest values? What will the brand never compromise on?
5. What is the brand's specific know-how? Its unique capabilities?
6. What is our brand's heritage, if any?
7. Where can the brand legitimately provide its benefit, in which territories and product categories?
8. Which products and actions best embody the brand's values and vision?
9. What are the brand's style and language, its stylistic idiosyncrasies?
10. What image does the brand want to convey of the customers themselves?

Brand purpose

Some people place an accent on the brand's specific point of view about the product category. This energizes the brand and justifies the brand's existence, its reason for being on the market, and provides it with a framework to approach the world.

For example, Dove rests on a major societal insight: most skin care brands foster an image of women that is male-centric (women are here to seduce and be nice). Instead, Dove addresses this by selling the self-worth of women. The company's goal is undoubtedly to generate profit and jobs, but its purpose is something else.

The notion of purpose was discussed earlier in the business strategy chapter. Brands derive their energy from their specific niche, vision, and ideals. To be able to lead the organization, the brand should be driven by an intense internal necessity.

There are two types of values to focus on in this connection: your core values – namely, the attributes that are necessary for the brand to remain itself – and the peripheral values – that is, traits that can show some flexibility.

Who decides the brand strategy?

Brad VanAuken believes that the brand strategy function should be the focus of the founder or leadership team of an organization. It is not a job for an outside designer, no matter how talented, and it is not the remit of your marketing team or social media manager either.[24]

Whatever the size of your business, thinking through your brand strategy is deeply connected to how you navigate the business itself. The brand strategy provides a route map for managing the development of the brand – and as such, this strategy belongs firmly with the leaders of the business. Get third party support to think through aspects of your strategy if necessary but do this thinking work *before* engaging a design

---

[24] www.brandingstrategyinsider.com/integrating-business-strategy-and-brand-strategy/#.YAuvWBanxdg

team to create your visual identity. As you will be working with a creative on designs anyway at the end of the process and covering strategy with them as part of their process, involve a broader base of expertise before the visual identity stage to decide your brand strategy. Then by the time you engage a designer you will have done much of your thinking work already, leading to a better visual design outcome.

In my view, businesses benefit from consulting people from different disciplines who have a solid understanding and experience of business, branding, and IP. Brand strategy has become one of those overused terms so that it can be difficult to know who is best placed to support your thinking on strategy. The fact is that strategists come from all sorts of backgrounds because branding involves many different disciplines. It may be that you would benefit from involving more than one strategist to help you with different aspects of your brand. For example, when it comes to your naming and distinctive brand assets I would suggest involving someone with a strong background in trademarks and IP who also understands branding. Do not assume this person should do the legal clearance and trademark registration work too. That can be left to your legal team to address. Their value in strategy goes beyond the work people traditionally associate with lawyers because their background experience in protecting brands provides a unique perspective on names and distinctive brand assets to help you to create a distinctive brand and ownership strategy.

Positioning: what do we want to stand for?

According to Phil Barden, even for high-consideration purchases people buy on emotion – that is, they will decide in system 1 and justify in system 2. So, it's desirable to inject emotion into your branding. Our emotions drive our behaviour because we are primarily goal oriented. So, if you are hungry and see an ad for food, that might drive you to buy that food, whereas if you have just eaten it will not motivate you to buy. On this basis, the aim is to consider what the category buyer is looking for and to position your offering in a way that is likely to be valued by some buyers so that they would be motivated to buy from you. That is the emotional connection to consider making.

While we focused on targeting and positioning in part 3 of the book, some companies may not have engaged marketing help to consider their positioning until they think through their brand strategy. So refer back to chapters 6 and 7, as these are equally relevant for establishing your brand strategy.

Brand promise

Additionally, bear in mind that your brand promise impacts your positioning.

The trust that your business gradually establishes in return for delivering a particular result or outcome, when customers buy from you, is how your business becomes known for a particular brand promise. Once your business is a recognized provider of a particular outcome that attracts customers to use you, your business becomes a trusted brand.

You will be known for delivering a particular quality or outcome because you have consistently and reliably done so in the past. Customers know what to expect if they use your product or service and there's little risk of an unpleasant surprise. Buying a product or service from a business that has not yet acquired trusted brand status is risky, because it represents something untried and untested. Once a business becomes recognized as a brand (even if only in a micro community), it can command a price premium or a market premium because some people will be willing to pay a premium to receive the expected results the brand is known for delivering. This applies even if the promise of the brand is based on price. For example, people may still prefer to shop at John Lewis rather than at an unknown online shop that has even better value product offerings, because they have certain reassurances regarding product quality and the shopping experience John Lewis promises. They will not have this comfort if they use an unknown seller. Shopping at John Lewis carries little risk because of the brand's promise of value for money and the fact that it is a trusted brand.

Your brand promise must be something you can realistically keep. Broken promises are among the three key reasons that brands fail:

1. They make irrelevant promises.
2. They over-promise.
3. They are inconsistent in delivery of their promise.

As you finalize how to articulate your brand promise out of the possibilities that are open to you, first find out what promises your customers want companies like yours to make and keep. Using the language that your customers use helps you to speak to them in a way that is relevant to them. Pay attention to how people express their desires and needs. Then look at your competition and at your own brand's strengths to decide which promises you can realistically make that would give you the best competitive advantage. The promise must address important consumer needs as well as leveraging your strengths.

The promise should be one that can give you a competitive advantage. It needs to be a benefit that is believable because it is effectively saying that only you deliver that benefit combined with a couple of others in your category.

For the brand promise to be clear to your consumers, it must be well understood by everyone in your organization, from the CEO to the receptionist. It must be manifest not only in consumer communication but also whenever and wherever the brand name and logo are used.

Think about how you will become known for the promise you want to be known for: which two or three things do you want the consumer to know about you – some people call this the brand essence, others, such as Kevin Keller, author of the popular book *Strategic Brand Management* (2019), call it the brand mantra.

Know how your brand is perceived

The two key pillars of your brand are your brand identity and brand positioning. Strategy will specify the path to follow to bridge the gap between the current brand image and the desired image that you decide in your brand strategy. By interviewing customers and key stakeholders, you can understand how your brand is currently perceived, and whether there are any problems that need to be addressed. Will you continue reinforcing how you are currently perceived, or does the business strategy suggest a need to pursue another goal for the brand? If so, how can you build on the customer trust your brand has already achieved so there is little risk of an unpleasant surprise when customers use you?

Brand tracking surveys are a useful way to find out how aware consumers are of the brand and whether they are customers; what they feel about your brand; what they expect from you and your competitors; and whether they plan to purchase your product or service. There are standard survey templates available from providers such as Survey Monkey[25] so there may be no need to develop your own surveys from scratch.

If you have a heritage, look back at your past. What have you learned that should be taken into planning the future?

Once you have refined your thinking, and decided what your promise should be, you can define your brand position in a way that is relevant to your target customer segment.

The following case study is instructive of how a sizeable company would tackle its brand strategy and tie it into its business strategy. It is reproduced by permission of Brad VanAuken, the author of *Brand Aid: A Quick Reference Guide to Solving Your Branding Problems and Strengthening Your Market Position* (2015). It involves a company in which he was employed as a brand manager.

Case study: Element K

Element K was an e-learning company which though quite substantial in size, discovered it had virtually no brand awareness among its target customers who were corporate chief learning officers. Their business strategy envisaged going public when the conditions were right. In the meantime, their objective was to quickly build brand awareness and differentiation and make the company the number one preferred e-learning brand.

The company's strategy was to target Fortune 1000 companies and large organizations because it had a

---

suitable solution, and the target audience was ideal because a substantial number of users came with each sales agreement.

Element K's research found that existing providers' messaging was inconsistent and commonplace. It consisted in explaining that the company had complete, integrated solutions, that their solution could improve your organization's performance, producing good business results, and that high-profile clients were pleased with their solutions.

Element K identified the key decision makers and the most powerful differentiating benefit for the company to claim because its interviews discovered people's needs, desires, fears, concerns, and other perceptions regarding training. Based on those insights the company developed some brand benefit statements which were refined through feedback from the target audience. In the process, they gained a major insight, namely that people have an underlying concern that, despite all its potential advantages, e-learning lacks the human touch. Element K happened to have a substantial advantage in addressing this fear because the business was naturally service-oriented as reflected in every aspect of the design and delivery of its solution. It was part of the DNA of the business which ran deep in every facet of the organization, including in the consultative selling style of its salesforce.

Bearing in mind the research findings about people's fears and Element K's strengths, as perceived by its customers, the company worked out its brand positioning.

Element K brings a unique understanding of how people learn to the business of training. Our understanding comes from a twenty-year heritage of innovation in adult career learning for leading corporations. Today, you'll find it in our best-in-class e-learning solution—over 800 courses integrated with a state-of-the-art learning management system, all delivered with a human touch.

The interplay between business strategy and brand strategy is evident in this case study, as is the need to do some further research beyond that which you might have done when thinking through your business strategy, to find out how your brand is perceived and how much awareness it has.

Marty Neumeier, in his book *The Brand Gap* (2005), discusses the gap that might exist between your brand strategy and the customer's understanding of your brand. When I asked him about this gap, he said:

What matters to a business is not what the company believes it's doing, but what the customers believe it's doing. Think of a business as a double helix. One strand of the helix is the business, and the other strand is the brand. Brand is how customers think of the business. If the two strands are not intertwined and connected up and down the helix, there's a disconnect. The DNA of your business is broken.

From Marty's comment it follows that you need to understand how your brand is perceived as a starting point to developing your brand strategy.

Creating a distinctive visual identity

Establishing your brand strategy helps you clarify the promise you want to communicate, and what story you might tell, what your messaging might be, and how to communicate it so the message lands. What will your brand personality be?

Your brand may enjoy great success due to its innovation or new product offering. Then, as copycats soon follow, the difference between your brand and that of your competitors disappears. This is why it is important to move swiftly when you launch your brand so you can take advantage of your point of difference before competitor copying diminishes your differentiation.

Once you have decided your brand strategy, articulate your requirements in a short one or two page document to brief a designer or agency to create your brand's distinctive visual identity. The various references in this book to leaving the visual design till the end of the process should not be taken as minimizing the importance of visual design in the branding process. Graphic design and visual identity is a hugely important part of branding. Great design goes beyond logos, typographies, and brand guidelines. Creative ideas, and the execution of your positioning, is a real skill. The visual designs should enhance and bring your brand to life, once you are clear what your purpose and positioning is. It is just that the order for doing this is to leave the visual designs till the end of the process.

Choose your team carefully, bearing in mind that there will be a variety of approaches to branding out there, and what you want is to find great designers to work with who are right for you. Ideally find a small project to work on with someone before entrusting your visual identity work to them. Your branding needs to maintain your market advantage once the inevitable happens and competitors pile in with similar offerings. Choose a designer to work with who will help you to create unique assets as part of your visual identity. Indeed, choose your brand name and brand assets guided by IP law. As designers and marketers are not intellectual property experts, involve an adviser in your team who understands branding and IP law to ensure your branding is legally distinctive and protectable.

Your brand elements, such as any icons you create to identify your brand, should be chosen with IP in mind so they can provide powerful protection for your underlying business concept. The way you communicate your offering needs to take account of the fact that there may be others offering the exact same thing. It will be your name and any visual symbol, logo, fonts, or other distinctive brand elements that will set you apart in the long run. Choose them so they are *unique* in your category. Avoid fashion trends because the objective of your logo design should be to stand out and avoid looking the same as everyone else's.

When it comes to visual designs, it is key to understand what IP can and cannot protect, and to be guided by what competitors have chosen for their visual identity so you separate yourself from the pack in unique ways to distance yourself from what the competition is using and has protected.

To be distinctive and unique with your branding involves looking carefully at competitors. Use a spreadsheet and track competitors by reference to their designs, their messaging, and their names. Then create a look and feel for your brand that is *completely different* to theirs. As mentioned in chapter 4, prioritize those brand elements that you will be able to protect from the outset. For colour, ownership may probably be more achievable if you use a unique approach such as using a combination of colours rather than relying on a single colour. However, remember that you will not be able to protect the brand's colour assets from day one so try to have a unique look and feel that could work regardless of colour, in case you need to change colours.

Choice of visual assets

In chapter 4, I described how I chose an owl to represent Brand Tuned only because it stood out. But just because the owl did not *come* from a meaningful story does not mean that it cannot *have* a meaningful story created for it!

To me, owls signify wisdom. A quick Google search tells me that they variously stand for paranormal wisdom, regal silence, and fierce intelligence. Owls are both great thinkers and hunters; they prefer to plan out their strategies instead of using brute force. I like the sound of this; it is perfectly possible to create a story around the owl that fits well with what I want Brand Tuned to stand for. I am sure I could have found other symbols if, for example, there were already a brand in the same space using an owl. Equally, I could have opted for a horse. According to Google, horses symbolize courage, freedom, power, independence, nobleness, endurance, confidence, triumph, heroism, and competition. I can see many relevant points here too with what Brand Tuned stands for and wants to represent.

My point is that it is possible to create a story around your choice of different brand symbols, and the same goes for brand names. There are a variety of options available when you are looking to design your visual identity. There is nothing that says one symbol and only one will do! Choose a designer or creative team to work with who understands what you are trying to achieve and can help you to create your desired distinctive look and feel. If, between you, you create a spreadsheet to capture the visual branding and messaging of your most significant competitors, you can ensure the visual identity that is created for you is distinctive and uniquely stands out in your category. Importantly, by protecting your brand assets and enforcing your rights against copyists, you can remain distinctive and unique long after competitors have copied your differentiation

Visual design work should be underpinned by the overriding need to stand out visually compared to existing competitors, and to choose distinctive brand elements that you can own immediately. This is key to ensuring your branding is distinctive. Be sure to set aside an appropriate budget for legal protection, rather than assuming that you automatically own the rights and that registration can wait. Protection is part and parcel of how you get a distinctive visual brand identity that is unique to you and is not mistaken for others. Protection is how you stop competitors copying your distinctiveness. You should expect competitors to try to look like you if you are successful. If you have not protected your unique brand elements you make it easier for them to create similar brand assets so that your visual identity becomes less distinctive. You will have then wasted the money you put into creating your distinctive visual identity!

Take home messages

- The leaders of the business are responsible for the brand strategy, with third party support if necessary.

- Articulate what the brand stands for and the promise it holds out to customers, identifying your top values and the brand's personality.

- Set out your brand strategy in a short brief for a designer or agency to create your brand's distinctive visual identity.

- Involve an adviser in your team who understands branding and IP law to ensure your branding is legally distinctive and protectable.

- Set aside an appropriate budget for legal protection, rather than assuming that you automatically own the rights and that registration can wait.

Part 5

tuned

Drive the brand strategy

In this part, we will look at how to use your branding consistently, and what it takes to become known in the ways you want to be known.

CHAPTER 12

Drive the brand strategy

Branding takes time to bed in. Once you have established your brand strategy and designed your visual identity, your ongoing efforts to build the brand should focus on one thing: to run the business in a way so you become known day by day for the two or three positioning elements you decided upon. The way you manage your brand should bear in mind the importance of how you treat customers and others and deliver your product or service. Think about minute details in how the business is run. Look at the various touch points of the customer journey to decide what you could do at each stage when delivering your product or service to reinforce your message to your target customers, so you become known in the ways you aspire to be known. This is how you stand a chance of becoming a trusted source for what your brand sells. You will need to convey and fulfil your implicit brand promise, so you become known for reliably meeting and delivering that promise. Think, too, of the internal aspects of the brand, which impact how you deliver your product or service, who you recruit, how you motivate and lead your business, so everyone is dancing to the same tune.

You will want to specify the marketing objective for your advertising, so that the brand develops in desired ways. Having clarity around what you want the advertising to achieve is critically important. Do you want it to increase brand awareness, attract new customers, increase brand loyalty, encourage add-on purchases, motivate people to switch from competitor brands to your brand, increase frequency of use, reinforce ongoing use, or what? Make sure the objective is quantifiable and measurable, as well as focused on two to three specific things you chose as part of your positioning strategy.

Your brand guidelines should be a resource insofar as they cover how to use the brand elements consistently in everything you do – advertising, marketing activities, internal communications, recruitment and hiring – everything. Consistency is about ensuring that each new exposure to the brand builds on the past, and your distinctive brand asset links strengthen in memory, making it easier for the category buyer to identify the brand in any situation.

Activate the brand

Once your brand is ready to launch, activate it by opening a dialogue with customers about your product or service offering, so you create an emotional connection and awareness that your new offering exists. People are often attracted to new things, so try to capitalize on that novelty value. Generating buyer interest about whatever your new product or service or business does is the heart of activation. Maybe you will launch by providing samples, to allow consumers to use your product or experience your service. Such experiential campaigns are designed to get people talking about the brand, so they form a strong impression of it early on. Getting exposure and media attention is key.

PR is often an important component of brand activation. It helps you work out how to attract press interest, so that one or more publications relevant to your target market run a story about the brand. Having a strong PR strategy in place ensures maximum coverage and helps give your brand a boost.

Bear in mind that brands are fluid and ever changing. Nothing stays the same. The paradox of branding is that you must change to stay consistent. Your ongoing efforts to build brand awareness should focus on becoming known for reliably meeting and delivering on your brand promise. It is about creating a unique and lasting presence in the marketplace, so the business operates in accordance with your values and becomes a trusted brand.

You need to communicate a consistent brand story, build community, and make an emotional connection to your audience. For example, many people have created communities by setting up shared interest groups or launched podcasts that have attracted like-minded people. Building communities is something that David Aaker and Kevin Keller (author of *Strategic Brand Management*) mention as important and desirable. In my own experience of the small business community, it is obvious that building communities is working very well for some businesses that manage to do it.

Consider the brand-building possibilities open to you when creating your marketing plan and decide how to allocate your budget between the various types of digital marketing and offline activities that you decide are relevant to your business, such as:

- Search engine optimization and content marketing
- Social media marketing
- Email marketing
- Paid advertising
- Networking, speaking, guesting on podcasts, and other offline methods

There are then three main issues to bear in mind as you build the brand:

1. Designing the total brand experience.
2. Ensuring your team are 'on brand'.
3. Doing both short-term and long-term marketing.

Designing the total brand experience

Consider the touch points in your customer's typical journey where they meet your brand. What could you do to add to the customer's experience of the brand at each point? How might you reinforce the brand promise in the way you handle customers?

If you have met your brand promise, but the customer was expecting something else, there is a mismatch between expectations, and customers will be disappointed. That is why it is critical to not just meet your own bar, but also to manage the customer's expectations. Depending on what you sell, it might involve asking the customer at the beginning of the process, even before they buy, a few questions to establish what they expect from the service. A book that helps uncover customer expectations so you can think about the expectations that are out of your control is *The Ten Principles Behind Great Customer Experiences (Financial Times Series)* (2012) by Matt Watkinson.

By connecting the dots, so that each customer experiences your brand promise in a positive way at each of these touch points, you can ensure you build a strong brand reputation and, ultimately, brand growth.

Surprise bonus

It is not just about meeting expectations – often, it is about exceeding them, by surprising the customer in a welcome way. Once you have got the basics down – meeting your brand promise at every touch point for every customer – think about how you might add an element of unexpected pleasure for the customer. According to Rory Sutherland, Vice Chairman of Ogilvy in the UK and author of the book *Alchemy: The Surprising Power of Ideas That Don't Make Sense* (2019), it is often the small things that count the most.

Watkinson also highlights a phenomenon known as the peak-end rule, which is about how our memory of an event is most influenced by how well or badly the experience ends.

Think about how you can make the final touch point both positive and memorable. To do this type of thinking for your brand on an ongoing basis Watkinson suggests making somebody senior within the organization responsible for the customer experience. It should not be someone attached to a particular department. The person should oversee the customer experience at multiple touchpoints and ensure consistency across the business.

Case study: Apple

One business that embodies the principles Watkinson advocates is Apple. The company has a relentless focus on the customer experience. Its brand value has been achieved through consistently creating products and services that work better than those of its immediate competitors. Apple employees are focused on ensuring customers leave the Genius Bar with their product working as it should, feeling well looked after.

The company's goal of designing the very best products it can, means Apple has created an enviable reputation for itself. As Sir Jonathan Ive, Apple's design head, put it: 'If we manage to do that then there are a number of consequences. People will like the product, hopefully they'll buy the product, and then we will make some money… The goal isn't to make money, the goal is to try to develop the very best product.'[26]

Ensuring your team are 'on brand'

To ensure that the experiences you design into the touch points of your customer journey reflect what you stand for and deliver as a brand, it is vital that your team should be 'on brand'. This starts with your internal communications. In an article in the

---

[26] 'Apple's Sir Jonathan Ive reaffirms desire to stay at company', *BBC*, www.bbc.co.uk/news/technology-18188670

Harvard Business Review in 2002,[27] Colin Mitchell says that by applying many of the principles of consumer advertising to internal communications, leaders can inspire employees. With a better understanding of the brand's vision, employees know how to 'live' the vision in their day-to-day activities. Customers are then much more likely to experience the company in a way that is consistent with its brand promise.

In Mitchell's view, employees should also be considered a 'market' much like buyers. You need to sell the brand to them, so they form an emotional attachment to the business' products and services. Explaining the brand promise to them ensures they row in the direction you are taking your brand. If you can 'sell' the brand to employees so they believe in the brand and its objectives, they are more likely to feel engaged. That then motivates them to work harder and their loyalty to the company increases. By uniting them around a common sense of purpose and identity you are more likely to achieve your business objectives and deliver your brand promise.

So, there is an element of the brand that is designed to inform the way you lead your organization. That requires a shift in the way you perceive employees. Rather than simply keeping them informed, you need to think in terms of selling it to them, convincing them of the uniqueness of the company's brand. So, it is vitally important to bring the brand alive for employees.

Therefore, not everything that you might think through when determining your brand strategy is designed to motivate buyers to choose to buy the brand. A large element of the brand, such as its mission (purpose) is about creating the internal culture,

---

[27] Colin Mitchell, 'Selling the brand inside', *Harvard Business Review*, https://hbr.org/2002/01/selling-the-brand-inside

one where workers are engaged and motivated to achieve the goal and mission of the business.

Having thought through your values and mission, consider how you will ensure your team embody and live the purpose. When hiring employees, ensure that they are a culture fit – aligning with your values and vision. Cementing your employer brand by creating the right kind of workplace so employees endorse your organization and help build the reputation you want to build, is key to a lasting brand. Your team need to embody and live the brand's purpose because everybody plays a role. Your mission should be aligned with the people you serve and your team. Make sure you communicate well so your team understand what it is they are expected to contribute and how they can live by your values. If your staff understand what you stand for and how they can help to achieve the brand's intended purpose, you will improve your chances of people outside the company understanding what the brand stands for.

Staff performance should be evaluated based on your purpose and values. Your staff and leadership team should understand the behaviours they need to display, how their performance will be evaluated, and the role they play based on your values and purpose. You are then much more likely to succeed in creating the right culture to support the business. This involves building a great company culture and infusing that culture into all areas of the company. Culture is not created just from putting up a sign on the wall or telling the world what it is you stand for on your website. How to ensure your team lives and breathes the brand values is detailed in an interesting book written by CEO of Zappos Tony Hsieh, *Delivering Happiness: A Path to Profits, Passion and Purpose* (2010). Hsieh speaks from experience of building a unique company culture to 'Deliver Wow' customer service; this is also Zappos' tagline, which underpinned their approach to delivering a world class customer service. This approach enabled the company to go from ailing online shoe sales company to US $1 billion in sales in less than 10 years. The company has now been acquired by Amazon.

Customer service may not be the core of your strategy, but there is much to learn from Zappos about how to build and create the right internal environment to support the brand values that are important to you and recruit the right team members. There are many other companies with strong employer brands, where team members are extremely happy. Glassdoor is a website that features the best employer brands each year. Google, Hubspot, and Salesforce are just three examples out of many that are featured there. What is clear is that nowadays it pays to build your brand as an employer to attract the right team members who can be motivated to deliver your brand promise.

Doing both short-term and long-term marketing

Let us recall Byron Sharp's evidence-based research that we considered earlier in the book. Byron Sharp found that the single biggest reason buyers choose one brand over another is that the brand has more physical and mental availability. This explains why Ford cars sell more than Renault cars everywhere except in France. More people think of Ford cars rather than Renault cars, not because they dislike Renault or because Renault lacks desirable features. It is simply that Renault cars are less well known, and hence fail to get a look in outside of France. They have less mental availability, in other words. So, the big issue in marketing is how to get your brand thought of more often, in more buying situations – how to build mental availability. In Renault's case, building more mental availability would ensure that their cars would get a look in, and that more people would remember to consider Renault cars when buying a car.

Buyers are 'polygamously loyal' as Sharp puts it. They have personal repertoires of brands they purchase repeatedly, but they are seldom 100% loyal, and are never exclusively loyal in the long term. This means that brands share buyers. How *much* they share depends on how effective other brands are at building their market share – their mental and physical availability. All brands in a category compete as if they were close substitutes, in spite of their physical or perceived differences. So, to ensure your brand is noticed when buyers are looking to buy what you sell involves marketing to the widest customer segments according to Byron Sharp's findings. This means building mental availability (awareness) so you become known. You must then ensure you are physically available in as many places as possible when consumers are looking to buy.

To do this, we should assume that customers lack imagination for the variety of contexts and circumstances in which our brand would suit their needs. Building mental availability is about developing different links in people's memories and refreshing those memory links in the brand's advertising and promotion. For example, Coca-Cola might run an ad campaign talking about drinking Coke when you are at the beach. The aim is that when people are next at the beach and want a drink, they will remember to buy Coke, not just have a drink. This goes beyond just raising awareness of Coke. It is raising awareness of how Coke might be relevant in a particular buying situation people may be in.

New brands should build the memories that consumers need to buy the brand, for example by communicating what the brand does, what it looks like, what the brand name is, where it is sold, and where and when it is consumed. These are simple but essential points to tell consumers and should inform your early marketing activities.

Marketing campaigns, then, should focus on one category entry point at a time and should tie in with any previous campaigns in order to build on them.

This is where Les Binet and Peter Field's work, *The Long and the Short* (2013), provides essential guidance. Their book establishes the principle that businesses grow most effectively when they allocate budget to both long- and short-term marketing. According to their findings, about 50%–60% of your marketing budget should be devoted to mass reach brand advertising, and the remainder should focus on narrowly targeted, segmented campaigns designed to generate immediate sales.

In other words, when marketing your business, you should target particularly relevant or interested buyers through messaging that can generate quality leads for your sales team and lead to a measurable Return on Investment (ROI). Otherwise, you will not attract sufficient sales – it is no good wasting money trying to target people who are not your customers for this purpose. So, you would just target your segment. However, we have seen from Sharp's work that you also need to reach all the people who could be involved in buying decisions over the longer term – if you focus purely on people who want your brand right now, you will miss all of the people who might want your brand in the future. This is about brand advertising.

As we have seen before, the same is true for product or service marketing as it is for brand marketing. Branding is a long game; the goal is to become well known for a particular position. Therefore, your brand marketing cannot be hyper targeted; it has to take the most inclusive possible view of your relevant audience and market to the entire segment. You hit immediate short-term goals with part of your budget to attract leads, and over time your long form of brand marketing will give you the short-term leads you need. If you are trying to build a brand for the long term, it is essential not to just target sales with your marketing activity.[28]

Take home messages

- At launch, open a dialogue with customers about your product or service offering, to create an emotional connection and trademark awareness of your new offering.
- Look at the touch points of the customer journey to decide what you could do at each stage to reinforce your message to your target customers.
- Sell the brand to employees so they understand the brand promise and are 'on brand' when communicating with customers.
- Make sure advertising objectives are quantifiable and measurable, as well as focused on two to three specific things you chose as part of your positioning strategy.
- Ensure you are physically available in as many places as possible when consumers are looking to buy.

[28] Mark Ritson, Les Binet, and Peter Field, 'The B2B marketing growth formula', LinkedIn Marketing Blog.

Epilogue

Branding is what turns a commodity into a brand. Take soap as an example: there is little difference between two soap products. It is due to branding that we make choices between different brands of soap and develop preferences for one brand over another. Branding is an important topic that I hope this book has made clearer while giving you insight into what to focus on to create your brand.

Remember that IP is a container of the brand equity. It is relevant when choosing or changing the identifiers by which a brand is recognized. The brand name, product names, slogans, and any codes such as colour, symbols, music, shapes etcetera all involve IP decisions. Ideally a brand management lawyer should be part of your team when these are being selected. Remember that brand protection impacts what is appropriate to create.

You need to understand yourself, your market, and the customer's problems to develop your brand. It is about having the empathy to know what it feels like to be in the customer's shoes facing that problem that your offering solves. As founder, your worldview shapes the brand so spend time thinking through your philosophy and values when deciding your brand strategy. Once you have decided what your brand stands for, and what promise you are willing to make (which is true to you, as well as something the market wants and needs), you can position your brand. Your positioning is what enables you to be more easily seen and bought and related to. It involves selecting two to three brand attributes to signal your brand and focusing your communications around these attributes so you are perceived in desired ways.

Your brand name and visual identifiers are the way your brand will be recognized and your hope is that consumers will associate your desired attributes with the brand as it develops mental availability. The clearer you are about the brand you are creating and how to distinguish it from competitors, the better your visual branding will be in uniquely identifying you. As we have seen, the brand name is a highly important decision. Also, it is crucial, once you have finalized your visual identity, not to change your designs, no matter how bored you might get with them. Their purpose is to enable consumers to recognize your brand.

Your logo and other brand identifiers should be registered as trademarks. If designers tweak them, you need to register new trademarks. This can get very costly especially where international trademarks are concerned, yet failing to update the trademark registrations impacts their enforceability. Engage creatives who understand the importance of choosing visual design elements that stand out in your industry, and who build on branding elements you already own, instead of seeking to change them when adding more brand codes. Choose designers who consider IP before finalizing the visual identity. That is how you create enduring distinctiveness.

The TUNED framework is applicable to any business of any ambition or size. How you use it to take account of IP and brand will be impacted by your ambitions for your business. If you are an ambitious founder, interested in building a substantial business and brand, you can assess what you need to do to better stand out as the first choice, or 'go to' brand, in your sector by taking the Brand Tuned scorecard test. It can be accessed here: www.brandtuned.com/scorecard.

What your business does, its values, its aspirations, how your business becomes known, all these details determine the brand you develop. It is important to manage your brand well, so enough people associate similar attributes with the brand.

This involves being very clear about what your brand stands for and represents, and managing your marketing budget to build the brand, not just to target sales. If you don't reinforce the brand's deeply held beliefs in your messaging when building awareness of the brand's positioning, you will have less success in the long run.

Do join the Brand Tuned newsletter at www.brandtuned. com/newsletter to find out more about how to manage your brand strategically. Your marketing shapes, develops, and communicates your products and services, as does your customer experience. The newsletter provides fortnightly updates and highlights useful podcasts that help in brand management.

I began this book with the aim of getting to the bottom of what is involved in creating a brand so I could understand why the branding industry treats brand creation separately to brand protection. I wanted to understand the issues and problems from the perspective of brand creation to explain why IP and brand protection considerations could and should support the objectives.

However, in my journey to this point in the book, I discovered a host of issues that I had not anticipated. I realized that there is much that the legal profession can and should do to better communicate the role of IP in branding. I believe we need a new discipline of brand management lawyer. There has never been more complexity in the global marketplace. The overlap between creative, commercial, regulatory, digital and legal considerations calls for a very different lawyer.

Currently people assume that they need an IP lawyer to support their branding but may not realize that IP lawyers include many different types of lawyer with different expertise that is not necessarily appropriate to brand management. Unless a lawyer specializes in trademarks and copyright they lack the basics to properly advise on branding projects. Company commercial lawyers, patent attorneys, copyright lawyers and others who have a general understanding of trademarks and offer trademark registration services lack the depth of knowledge needed in branding. Trademark lawyers have some of the necessary skills but need to upskill themselves to manage the increasing complexity branding entails in a global internet environment. The upshot is that the public sometimes get questionable value when they consult IP lawyers. No wonder people have come to assume that the only purpose of a lawyer during branding is to search and register trademarks! Now that Intellectual Property Offices around the world make it easy for anyone to register trademarks, it would seem you don't even need a lawyer for trademark registration either. This could not be more wrong.

Another discovery that I had not expected when I set out to write this book, was the confused and muddled state of branding as a discipline. Nor did I envisage the controversies that exist around concepts like differentiation and brand purpose. Writing the book had its challenges as a result.

I drew conclusions based on what made sense to me intellectually about the evidence-based research of the Ehrenberg-Bass Institute. I looked for guidance from people who were taking Sharp's research on board in their own approach. I continue learning as I conclude this book having discovered formal training programmes in brand management and marketing that I've now signed up to. And my knowledge of branding is increasing thanks to books I'm reading, my podcast and the work I do with clients.

I welcome hearing from readers. Please do reach out to me at shireen@brandtuned.com and let me know what worked, what didn't, and how I might support you. What ideas did the book trigger in your head, what results did you have, was there something that was missing that you would have appreciated more of? I would love to know so I can write blogs or record podcasts to plug any gaps. If you benefit from the book, it would mean the world if you would take a few moments to leave a review. Thank you so much if you do!

About the author

Shireen Smith is the founder of Brand Tuned, a brand consultancy that supports companies to define and develop their brand and to position themselves for the 21st century. A key area of her work is advising on the IP aspects of branding, in particular on how to identify and protect names and how to stand out using protectable IP assets.

Her interest in business and entrepreneurship led her to move to in-house positions at Coopers & Lybrand and then Reuters after qualifying as a solicitor. She took a few years away from the workplace to raise her two daughters and trained as a journalist and completed a master's degree in intellectual property. She then briefly returned to private practice, working at the international law firm Eversheds, before founding IP law firm Azrights and focusing on IP, specifically on trademarks and brands.

She speaks and blogs on branding and IP, and provides consultancy on branding through Brand Tuned, where she also offers an Accelerator programme for ambitious entrepreneurs that want to be the authoritative brand in their sector.

Contact:
info@brandtuned.com

www.linkedin.com/in/shireensmith/
twitter.com/ShireenSmith
www.instagram.com/shireensmith/
www.facebook.com/shireensmith.4

www.linkedin.com/company/brand-tuned/
twitter.com/brand_tuned
www.instagram.com/brandtuned
www.facebook.com/brandtuned

Index